Continental Giant Rabbit Concerns

Health Matters

Author: Eva M. Wells

Continental Giant Rabbit Concerns: Health Matters

The material contained within this book is not intended as veterinarian or other such medical advice. If your pet has a medical issue, consult a qualified professional.

Copyright © 2020 by Eva M. Wells - Continental Giants in USA - 1st Choice Hypnosis

Continental Giant Rabbit on book cover: "Cooper", owned by Hannah Nolasco of Louisiana, USA, other photos and rabbits contained within this book are owned by Eva Wells and Renate Strosahl and Evelyn Walsh

Editor: Jane Schreiner

Proofread by: Sara Everhart

All rights reserved.

Published by 1st Choice Press in the United States of America

ISBN: 978-1-7353891-5-8

Printed in the United States of America.

All rights reserved. No part of this publication may be reproduced, distributed, or transmitted in any form or by any means, including photocopying, recording, or other electronic or mechanical methods, without the prior written permission from the author, except in the case of brief quotations embodied in critical reviews and certain other non-commercial uses permitted by copyright law.

First Printing: January 2021

Portions of this book were originally published as various rabbit related website content and blogs, and other literary material created by Eva M. Wells in 2014 - 2020.

Eva M. Wells, CPH, CMLC
1st Choice Hypnosis
115 W. Main St.,
Eaton, OH. 45320

www.continentalgiantusa.com

www.1stchoicehypnosis.com

Eva M. Wells is available to speak at your event on a variety of topics. Send email to: continental.giant.usa@gmail.com for booking information.

Why Read This Book

This book offers you the viewpoints and suggestions researched, gathered, and experienced by one of the first Continental Giant owners in the United States, as well as other breeders. You will also receive advice and tips which cover the enter life span of these amazing giant rabbits, conveniently, all in one place.

Most of the information can be adjusted for use in most all other rabbit breeds. Additionally, you will discover long-time breeders' secrets on how to provide the best care when it comes to how to recognize, what to do, and what your options may be for raising, caring for, and helping your Conti maintain the healthiest life possible. Plus, there are many more nuggets that you will be thrilled to have on hand.

What others are saying...

"... these books are my Rabbit Bible!"

"... even those who are experienced with this breed needs to read these books."

"... people who do not properly prepare for the animal of their dreams by taking the time to learn everything they can before taking it home are repeatedly disappointed."

"...it is in your best interest to take this opportunity to rad and digest the information found in (her) books."

"Eva taught me exactly how fragile they are compared to the Flemish and other breeds."

"... your books are truly a godsend to those new to the breed."

"... even someone experienced with rabbits needs to read these books as the Conti will require a different level of care..."

"Don't enter into this relationship (of owning Conti) without first reading this book."

"... packed with essential information for anyone looking to acquire, integrate, and care for a Continental Giant rabbit."

Continental Giant Rabbit Concerns Health Matters

TABLE OF CONTENTS

ONE : We All Want the Best 1

TWO : Inside Out 9

THREE : Teeth 14

FOUR : Eyes 22

FIVE : Ears 26

SIX : Feet 40

SEVEN : Brains, Organs, and Bones 48

EIGHT : Digestive Disorders 54

NINE : Nutrition 63

TEN : Reproduction 69

ELEVEN : Fur 75

TWELVE : Personality 79

THIRTEEN : Medicine 85

FOURTEEN : Final Thoughts 95

BONUS SECTION 101

ONE
We All Want the Best

Who wants to have the healthiest rabbit possible? Or, perhaps the better question would be to ask, who wants a sick rabbit? Not me; nor anyone else that I know of. Who would? Especially when you are investing in a big giant bunny that you have spent a considerable amount of time in finding a breeder, waiting until the breeder has a litter born, then waiting to be able to choose one, spend more time in picking out a name, getting excited and waiting weeks to months later for that baby to be old enough to leave it's mom, and then investing in either a trip to pick up or finding a transporter who will pick up and deliver to you. Not only does all of this take a considerable amount of time, but it also costs a very pretty penny to get to this point. So, after all of this, and once your excitement has grown and you finally get your new baby home, not to mention that by then you have already become emotionally attached. No one in their right mind would be happy to end up with a baby that gets sick, or worse, dies within a couple of weeks of getting him. Just the opposite happens; you are heartbroken, or at the very least, really upset and if we are going to be honest, you're likely also going to be quite angry. If the bunny was for your child, well, that only doubles the upset, doesn't it?

Unfortunately, however, sometimes that is exactly what happens. This is not to say that the breeder was at fault either. The fact is that all breeders want to produce and provide others with the best baby possible. It feeds their ego, and their heart swells with joy to know that their own investment of time and money will go on to live a happy life. That is how breeders make a name for themselves; by passing along healthy, sweet, beautiful babies. The last thing they want is to get a call, telling them that the baby is sick – or had just died. Sadly, also, most breeders do not have a reserve stock-pile of babies on hand either, so they typically do not have the ability to readily send you a replacement. They also understand the fact that their own four months-worth of caring, nurturing, loving, and raising that baby just got flushed away as well. When you look at it like that, you can clearly see that in such a case everyone loses.

As if that wasn't bad enough, you can then combine the fact that not only do most breeders not have the ability to instantly replace your new baby, but then they are faced with what else can happen. This is why almost every breeder has a sales policy in effect. They don't have one because they expect problems; they have one because they know that anything can happen, at any time, and there can be dozens upon dozens of reasons why bad things happen. First, they have no idea what happens with the baby once it is removed from their care. Perhaps it was just a fluke, or perhaps not. They simply have no way to know. Did the baby eat something toxic? Did the baby come in contact with another rabbit, or some other animal, that could had been sick? Was there some weird issue that was already going on, that they honestly did not know about? Did the buyer follow through with feeding and care instructions? Was there mold or something else wrong with the feed given to that baby? How stressed did the baby become because of being moved, and during transport? Did the buyer allow the bunny to roam around freely in the vehicle during transport and it possibly got injured that way, somehow? The questions are many, and the answers are unclear. Even after receiving a full explanation of the situation from the buyer, without meaning any offense to anyone – buyer or breeder – there is also no guarantee that any little detail could had been missed, overlooked, or even accidentally misrepresented, by either party, and of course there are always those situations where one truly is unaware of an issue. It does happen, and it happens more often that what is usually realized. The plus side of that, however, is that even though it may not be good information, any and all information is good to learn. Even if something cannot be changed about the current situation, it helps prevent the same type scenario from helping again, in the future.

So, what do you do when something goes wrong? Obviously, your first option is to respectfully and peacefully try to work something out with the other person. Perhaps an offer of a future-replacement can be given. If it's a genetic issue, that replacement could be offered from a different lineage, if possible. And yes, there is the option of refunding. The vital and most important factor here is that, from a breeders standpoint, any options should be thought of in advance and noted in some form of a sales policy. Doing this provides the buyer with information of what to expect, just in case something does go hay-wire, and it helps ease the panic of 'oh no! Now what am I going to do?' on the buyers end. Additionally, it clears up a whole lot of possibilities from the beginning of the arrangement made. There is a catch to all of this of course. In order for any arrangement to be carried out, each person involved must be aware of what is on the line before they even make the first deposit, if a deposit is required, to reserve the baby in question.

Sales policies do not have to be stringent. In fact, the only thing they need to cover is what is being offered, what you are and are not willing to provide at the price agreed upon, and what your contingency plan is, in case something turns sour. Examples of things that should be included could include, but does not have to be limited to options based on the following questions:

- Is a minimum deposit required / how much if so?
- What if the buyer only pays a partial amount of the deposit and then later comes back and wants a refund?
- How long does the buyer have to pay the deposit or balance once they ask to buy the rabbit in question?
- Will payments be accepted, or is the basis done for a deposit and balance due at pick-up?
- Will there be any transitional feed, hay, and/or water sent with the rabbit at the time it is picked up?
- What forms of payment are acceptable?
- Who will be responsible for finding and arranging transportation of the rabbit from breeder to buyer?

- Will there be any type of care-guide offered to the buyer, at the time of pick up?
- Does the breeder and buyer only agree to working with one type of transport? Such as airline travel, for example
- Does the breeder require the buyer/transporter to have and show a specific type of transport carrier at the time of pick-up?
- Is there any type of health guarantee for the life of the rabbit?
- If there is any type of health guarantee, how long is the time frame being offered?
- What are the buyer's options if the rabbit dies within x-amount of time?
- Will the breeder accept any responsibility for any vet fees incurred once the rabbit leaves their possession?
- Does the breeder accept any type of liability for any injury caused after the rabbit leaves their possession?
- How long is the breeder willing to hold the rabbit in their possession if the buyer is unable to follow through with the originally agreed upon pick-up date?
- If the breeder is willing to hold the baby for x-amount of time after original date of pick-up, is there a fee for boarding and care until another pick-up date can be arranged?

- If the buyer backs out, once the deposit is made, will the breeder refund any of the deposit paid?
- What options will be made if the buyer arrives to pick up the rabbit and finds the rabbit to be not what they expected or wanted?
- If the buyer is not satisfied with the rabbit, is the breeder willing to take the rabbit back?
- If the breeder takes the rabbit back, will there be any form of restitution – choice of replacement, refund, etc.?
- Does the breeder require the buyer to return the rabbit to them, free of charge and no replacement offered, if the buyer can no longer keep the rabbit for any reason?
- Is the buyer free to re-sell the rabbit to anyone if they cannot keep or no longer want the rabbit for any reason?
- Is there a non-breeding agreement in place for rabbits with genetic deficiencies?

As you can see, the list can be long, and there can be any variation of other scenario's included in, added to, or deleted from the above questions. The point being made, however, is that both the buyer and the seller needs to understand what they are dealing with, up front. Additionally, any type of agreement should be posted publicly so that anyone can see what they are dealing with, before they decide on purchasing a rabbit from said-breeder. Doing this will save everyone involved a lot of time and trouble. I will also note here, unfortunately, there are a whole lot of 'sue-happy' people in this world. Therefore, having all of your priorities, arrangements, agreements, and offers spelled out in black and white can absolutely cover your back in case you find yourself at the hands of one of these threats of being sued, as well as it being your 'preventative' for being stabbed in the back when someone decides they do or don't want something that they did not originally agree upon.

TWO
Inside Out

I'm sure you have heard the cliche, "it's in our genes", well, when it comes to health, that is exactly where it begins. We all know that when a problem arises, you need to start at the very beginning in order to find the solution. Nothing is truer when it comes to the genetic make-up of the species that is in question. Hundreds of problems begin at a cellular level. It's scientifically proven, and undeniable. Every molecule that is banded together connects to others and as the process continues, structure is formed. When something is out of sequence however, regardless of what that structure is, formation is not completed correctly and hence, 'Houston! We have a problem!'.

When the groundwork is faulty, only one result can occur. There will be a deficiency that grows, and at some point, then becomes a deformation. That deformation can present in many ways. For the purpose of this discussion, we will keep it at a minimum; in other words, without responsible breeding tactics and utilizing the maturity of breeding selectively and culling the undesirable traits, those problems only multiple and worsen. By choosing to ignore, avoid, and disregard the facts that these genetic problems exist, and if you 'breed it anyway', you – friend – are part of the problem of why these problems are very close to reaching a boiling point. We all know what happens when the boiling point starts, right? The pot boils over, and incidentally, someone(s) always ends up getting burned.

I have said it before, but fully repeating it here, again: if you think it is ok to sweep genetic problems under the rug, it will come back to bite you – hard. The reason is simple. No one likes to or wants to be taken advantage of. By breeding and then selling 'hush-hush' style while thinking no one will find out, well, let's just be honest, people talk! Rabbit breeders are absolutely notorious for doing exactly that, and it only takes one bad situation knowingly done to ruin your name as a breeder. This is not to say that sometimes the breeder is being upfront and honest and truly was unaware there was a problem. The difference between the two though is that the unaware breeder who is trying to learn from the experience and do better will then stop in their tracks, cut the losses, cull the line, and then move on; the breeder who is out to make the next buck (pun intended) will continue breeding the unhealthy lines and further passing them along to other unsuspecting buyers. The results will play out as being that you will either gain the respect of other responsible breeders by being upfront and honest, or you will be out-cast and smeared through the mud as someone who rips people off. I'm sure I don't have to tell you how long you will last, or how far you will get, if that is your preference; especially when there's a high dollar attached to the scenario.

Obviously, the choice is yours. No one can rightfully tell you what to do with the rabbits that you bought and now fully own. However, I say all of the above in hopes that you will make the decision to do what is right – for the rabbits and for those who do. Unfortunately, yes, that might mean that you will end up eating a bit of expense if someone puts you in that place (which obviously would be the case, if this applies to you). If that happens, I am truly sorry that you had to experience that. No one should have to. If everyone would be honest, this wouldn't even be mentioned. With that not being the base though, the best thing that we can do is to move on in a way that we can at least hold our own heads up-right and feel good about what we are doing, and who we are in regard to being 'a decent human being, trying to improve the breed', so to speak. Beyond that point though, I am not – in any way – "the bunny police". I am not trying to dictate what you do or what your breeding practices are. My entire point is only to say that by being responsible and taking action, you will be doing a great service to the Continental Giant community as a whole, and you will gain the respect of being a good breeder in return. That, in and of itself, will open a lot of doors for you in the future.

Perhaps you are wondering, especially if you are new to all of this, just exactly what types of genetic problems are involved with this breed. So, I will explain. The most common issues are malocclusion (bad teeth), a lopped ear, and various organ diseases. Each of these areas will be covered in depth, in their own chapters. So, I will let that go at that, except to note that I do suggest that you not only skim over those chapters, but that you fully read them and commit to learning them. Doing so will only improve your understandings of why these problems continue to exist and how they can be eradicated. To eradicate them, of course, it is vital that everyone who reads these (and those) words and takes them as the valuable knowledge in which that they are intended for, and then choosing to implement them in your Conti lines.

Some of you may also may be wondering what you can do if you are the one who has to discover the hard way that there are genetic problems in your own lines. Not everyone is in agreement of doing a hard-cull (euthanize), yet you also do not want to just continue spreading the problems and pushing it off on someone else to deal with. This is what is referred to as "soft-culling". Basically, there are a couple options. First, you can keep the inflicted bunny(s) as your own pets. Next, you can choose to have those inflicted spayed / neutered, and then sell them as pets. And third, you can take the risk of selling and trusting your buyer to carry out the spaying/neutering and not ever breed him/her. I would, at the very least, suggest that if you go with the third option, then do not provide any form of a pedigree with that bunny(s), do not disclose anything particular about the parents of that bunny(s), and to also clearly tattoo the ear as being "PET ONLY". On a side note, just to cover your own backside, I would also not release the bunny(s) without the buyer signing an agreement saying that they have fully been told and understand that rabbit does carry a genetic problem and that they agree to never breed him/her, for any reason. By doing that, if someone later comes back to you and says that this problem exists because of you selling a rabbit with known problems, then you have signed papers stating that you did your due-diligence and are not in any way responsible for what that person did. That releases you from further liability, and prevents the risk of having your name ruined. Additionally, even if you are dealing with a person that you have known a while and trust, chances are very high of that person selling you out just as quickly as anyone else (especially if they are jealous, mad, or aiming to get ahead). So, trust no one and be honest with everyone, then you will have no worries.

THREE
Teeth

Continental Giants have large, powerful teeth. Like all rabbits, they have a total of 28 teeth, which appear in 3 rows. The ones we see are the front row, which is the front upper and lower 4 teeth. Next, there are 4 other teeth, known as 'peg teeth', located slightly behind the front ones. Then there are the back teeth, which are used for grinding up food. In between these front and back rows of teeth is a space which is where un-chewed food can be stored while they continue eating. These teeth, all, grow constantly. For this reason, they must be ground down continuously. This happens by eating the proper food and chewing on wood and other such materials. Additionally, teeth may fall out on their own, either by damage, infection, excessive use, injury, or genetic cause. If any fall out on their own, they will regrow as long as there is not a serious health issue involved.

Ideally, the teeth should come together and meet in place when the rabbits' mouth is not open. If any teeth are shorter than others, this can affect how they chew their food, and if the teeth are longer than others, crooked, split or gaped apart, not only can the rabbit not chew their food but they can also cause significant problems to the gums, cheeks, and lips. This is typically also your first indication that you may be dealing with malocclusion. While it is possible that malocclusion can occur due to an injury, or even an incorrect diet, it is not common for that to the be case. Most often, the problem is genetic! That means it is hereditary. This is what we are going to focus on in this chapter.

Although to the best of my knowledge it is scientifically unproven, it is believed that malocclusion began due to cross-breeding incompatible rabbits. For instance, if you breed a rabbit that has a skull structure which is short and round to another rabbit with a skull structure that is long and narrow, the offspring will carry both genetic variances which can result in babies with unequally balanced jaw bones. As I just noted above, rabbits have different sets of teeth because they each perform separate duties. The front teeth bite and tear, the pegged teeth behind those separate and divide, and the back teeth then grind and chew. If all of the teeth, combined, are not meeting together to form a correct bite, then the food cannot be chewed properly, the misaligned teeth – because they continuously grow- then cannot be ground down to the size required for use. Instead, his further can result in infection, decay, and more significant mouth trauma caused by those teeth which will continue growing to the point that they can and will injure the other areas of the mouth. All of the above also causes the rabbit to be unable to eat, which obviously then becomes fatal.

There is no known test that can be done to determine congenital malocclusion, and furthermore, the exact known gene(s) responsible for this severe problem are unknown as well. Because of these reasons, the only option to identify carriers is by testing the water. This means that unless you already know that there has been one or more inflicted with bad teeth, then all you can do is breed and pay attention. It is common for bad teeth to noticeable around 3 weeks of age, however, that is not always the case. Sometimes, it takes several months. It has even been suggested that until a rabbit is past 6 months of age, the risk is still eminent. Once you are at or beyond 7 months of age, the risks of occurrence are slim to none. I am not a Vet, so I can't guarantee these statistics – however, from all of my experience combined, I do agree with them and have not found reason to believe otherwise. On the flip side though, I have learned that this little genetic mess is very unpredictable! There could be several generations without a single issue showing up and then, out of the blue, it absolutely will rear its ugly head once again.

The next question that I am sure most of you are asking is what do you do if you do the breeding, even to the point of having previously bred the same buck and doe and have had no problem, and then bam! Bad teeth appear. This is where I refer back to the options of what to do with offspring, either via hard or soft culling and ensuring all those from that lineage are not bred again. Even if there are other babies in the litter that appear to have good teeth, you now know, without a doubt, that those litter-mates are malocclusion carriers. There is no denying it! That means that if you sell them to someone else and that person breeds them, you just played a role in passing the problem along to others. If this is coming from a mating that had been done before and that prior litter was sold without known problem, well – to add insult to injury, per se, not only should you never breed that buck and doe together again, but you should go back and contact prior buyers and inform them of what has been discovered, so they too can act accordingly in their own breeding programs and save themselves the headache and torment of having to also find out the hard way. No! It is not pleasant by any means for anyone to have to do all of this. No one wants to hear it, and no one wants to deal with it. Choosing to ignore it and sweep it under the rug, however, is just wrong and it is unethical! Still though, no one can tell you what to do – but hopefully, you will do what is right.

At one point, when the Conti were new to the United States, tracing malocclusion was easily done and record was kept, by myself and others. However, within the last 2-3 years, so many imports have been brought into the country and there are so many USA and import lines that have been sold, and many new breeders added as well, that tracking it all has basically turned into a lost cause, of sorts, to even try to keep track it all. Even though this also does increase the availability of Continental Giants and eases the job of finding one. However, that also means that the genetic problems have more than quadrupled, and its fairly safe to say that is saying it lightly. Yes, this means that the once believed 'safe lines' that meant healthier offspring now is not always the case; as there are problems reported in many lines, regardless of origin.

To make tracing a far uglier problem, for the past couple of years, breeders have entirely failed to create proper pedigrees and others have passed along faked ones (unknowingly, I'm sure). This is not said to point fingers, but it is the truth and I offer no apology for it. For years, I tried to teach others that is it vital that they learn how and actually follow thru with properly filling out a pedigree. Many ignored it and still do. The bottom line here folks, is that those pedigree's provide answers! Those answers would had gone a long way in saving us all when it comes to tracing bloodlines. But, because people chose to ignore and do their own *incorrect* formatting of pedigrees, now, there is no easy way to keep track of what is what, where it truly came from, and how to effectively eradicate this problem – without so many Conti suffering needlessly, and dying. Tracking can still be done, don't get me wrong. To do so though would take an extreme amount of time, work, energy, and effort though. Honestly, to my best knowledge, there is probably no one willing to do the work to make it happen. Doing so would require multiple years' worth of every breeding done by every breeder in the nation to also be willing to be honest in claiming and accounting for every single Conti they had a hand in producing. I'm sure you can imagine, with that said, how virtually near impossible that would be to accomplish. If someone wishes to attempt it though – well, good luck! I wish you the best. Furthermore, if this is you, by all means contact me personally and I will be glad to talk with you about the original information that I have. Otherwise, if there happens to be even one person who wants to do the right thing and correct the pedigree problems; start out by signing your work! That means if you produced it and are honest and proud enough to let it leave your possession, you should be equally proud enough to attach your rabbitry or barn-name to each and every one that you do create and send out and to put your handwritten signature to it if possible. If you don't understand that, it means that when you are creating pedigrees for your babies, where you enter the baby's name, title it. For example: the format of "Ginger" is wrong! ... to be correct, you should be writing the pedigree as "ACME's Ginger". Then, you are legitimately and permanently known as the breeder of that rabbit.

To wrap up this section, I will just say that to the best of my knowledge, malocclusion cannot entirely and fully be bred out. It must be culled out. The reason is because once you breed a known carrier, everything that is produced from that rabbit is then also a carrier. Even though you may not breed it to another known carrier, everything you sell from the carrier-litters that are sold will continue producing carriers, and eventually someone will breed to another carrier and the ballgame starts all over again. This is why it is so important to not just sweep the problem under the rug and act as if it does not exist, or otherwise choose to ignore it. That does happen, unfortunately, and probably happens a lot more often than what most people would think possible. Each and every single time it is repeated, the problem will only continue getting worse and worse. Again, this is not said to be pointing fingers at anyone, at all. It simply is the truth and there is nothing that can change the nature of this genetic beast; at least nothing known of at this time, and I would be hard-pressed to believe it will happen any time in the near future, too. Trust me, you do not want your name associated to this issue. As big of a loss, and as hard as you may find it to do, you will gain far more respect as a breeder by doing it. Not to mention, you are saving yourself the headaches that will come back to bite you later on, once your name becomes part of the not-talked-about blacklisted names of the "Mal-Breeders" list – the ones that everyone else who has even half of a clue of what they are doing who will go far beyond out of their way to stay away and warn others to stay away from anything with your name attached to it.

FOUR
Eyes

While Continental Giants do not seem to be bombarded with eye problems, there are some that do pop up from time to time. Therefore, they are worth including, because as always, it's best to be over-prepared and not need it than to run into an emergency and not be prepared.

The most common issues that bunny owners have are eye infections, better known as Conjunctivitis, Tear Duct Disease (Dacryocytitis), Glaucoma, Abscesses, Tumors, and related issues due to RHVD, RHVD2, and Pasteurella, and of course, injury.

Starting with the related issues, these issues, along with Conjunctivitis (pink eye), are often caused by a bacterial infection which has become chronic. All of which involve an infection which effects the mucous membranes, causing the infection to spread to the eyes. The other conditions are mainly caused by dental problems which result in the eyes being affected. The tricky part here is to figure out which problem you are dealing with. Then, you will be able to choose the best plan of action towards treating and, hopefully, fixing the problem.

In addition, it will be helpful for you to understand the parts of the eye.

- OPTIC NERVE: this is the nerve that connects the brain to the eye and results in the ability to see
- RETINA: the part of the eye where a layer of cells at the back of the eyeball sends and receives signals to the brain, thru the optic nerve, which results in the images we view
- LENS: inside the eyeball, this tiny round shaped structure is what allows us to have the focus of an image, to send and receive the information through the retina, into the optic nerve, and then to the brain
- PUPIL: a tiny hole in the iris which allows light to enter, providing us with the ability to differentiate various parts of images
- IRIS: the round part of the front of eye that is colored

- CORNEA: this is a thin layer that covers the eye, and coincidentally is most easily damaged
- CONJUNCTIVA: the pink tissue in and around the eye and eyelid
- EYELID: rabbits have 3 parts of an eyelid - the upper, lower, and 3rd eyelid. The upper and lower eyelids are considered as the outer-eyelids, while the 3rd eyelid is located in the corner, underneath the outer-layers of the eyelid.

The symptoms you will notice, if there's an eye infection, are most often scratching, redness, swelling, watery or runny eyes, and discharge. In addition to these symptoms, you could also notice some 'crusting' in the corner of the eyes. The only way to absolutely know without a doubt what condition you are dealing with, you will need to have an exotic Vet to do an exam. As noted above, to get the best results from treatments, you need to know exactly what you are dealing with.

If you find yourself in a pinch, however, there are multiple treatment options for infections. Vetericyn is an antimicrobial product that you can get over the counter or order online. It is widely used & recommended; there are claims are that it is effective for Conjunctivitis, as well. You can find it in a spray or in gel form, plus it is quite cheap to buy. It is also fairly easy to get; as Tractor Supply Stores, Petco, and other major animal-based stores carry it on the shelves. Others' recommend Terramycin,

FIVE
Ears

Another genetic problem in Continental Giants, which is spreading at an alarming rate, is passing along babies with a lopped ear. Breeders are selling these one-ear wonders like water pouring through a net. Sure, there are several reasons why an ear could lop, and we will discuss them in this chapter, but that does not excuse the fact that the problem is so widely ignored that it has reached the point of burning like a wild fire out of control. Equally, as such a wild fire would destroy everything in its path, this genetic anomaly outright wreaks havoc where-ever it goes. This is in part because those who are producing babies with lopped ears often do not understand the exact cause of what they are dealing with, and as such, they think it is no big deal, or in some cases, they honestly don't care. It is for the first grouping, along with buyers, that I am creating this list.

The 1st case: Could be but HIGHLY UNLIKELY caused by injury to the ear base. ONLY believe this theory if the accident was witnessed, or if you have x-ray showing the damage, or if it occurs in an older, mature Conti which up until that point had perfect ear carriage.

The 2nd case: somewhat common in young Conti, up to the age of about 5months. This is due the growth & development changes in the cartilage surrounding the ear (the ear base) and also is affected by heat (aka a form of "summer ears"). These situations can & will self-correct in time, typically by the time the baby reaches 5 months of age, as the skull & cartilage development becomes more mature. I will note here, too, that some breeders do not believe this theory. I'm not here to convince you one way or the other, either. I'm merely pointing out information; what you opt to do with that information is entirely up to you.

The 3rd case: This is the worst of possibilities, which begins with an ear base that is weakened due to breeding with poor quality genetics, and/or the continued practice of cross-breeding Conti to a lop-eared breed of rabbit, most commonly the French or English Lop. This can and will cause weak ears & it will be genetic. There is a good and a bad side to this, also. We will begin with the good news, as it this condition offers a point of correction with subsequent breeding to the destination-breed, with high quality specimens, which will re-strengthen the ear base. In other words, this weakness can be "bred out" by repetitively breeding back to either a Flemish Giant, or a Conti with strong ear-base and having no lineage known of previous cross-breeding in those lines which included a lop-eared breed.

The bad news, on the other hand, is that the Continental Giant as a breed is believed to had included in the creation of the breed, at some point during the earlier parts of the breed becoming a breed, by selectively breeding a Flemish Giant to a French Lop, which further is complicated due to the fact that the French Lop was originally created by crossing a Flemish Giant to English Lops. In essence, what has happened is basically a 2-to-1 Ruling based on a lop structure bred to a non-lop structure. Further complicate that, then, by understanding that the practice continues today. In fact, it is known that reason the German Grays, or German Giants, have such a big boxy-looking head appearance because they were and are somewhat routinely bred back to French Lops, to maintain the more desired "bull-dog" look which they are most well known for having.

Other than that, the cross-breeding situations are often done for new color development and, oddly enough, improved ear structure, to achieve extended length and width. If you are working on such a project as a breeder, be ethical and honest, upfront, and explain the cross breeding with the possibility of a faulty ear condition. Note here, too, that such babies should not be sold to another breeder, at all. They should be soft-culled, which means kept or sold as pets – without pedigree or specific lineage information, and a non-breeding agreement is often suggestive to be signed, with the buyer agreeing that they are aware of the genetic risks, stating that breeding will not occur, and that they will have that rabbit spayed or neutered as soon as their vet will agree to doing the procedure. Just to cover your back, I would state that you are in no way liable or responsible for that rabbit once it leaves your possession.

I will also warn you, before going any further, that the following information is possibly going to upset a lot of Conti owners. The best thing I can say in response is that upsetting anyone is not the intent, at all. In no way, shape, or form is this an attempt to cause anyone to feel bad or upset, nor is it meant to be taken as any sort of finger-pointing. Quite the contrary, really. The intent is purely and only informationally based, with the purpose of educating and the hope of saving a lot of bunny-lives. Furthermore, I have thoroughly dug into this situation and have been researching and reading everything I can get my hands on, during the last year, and I have been working with several others behind the scenes to get a grip on this ordeal and come up with a manageable option to possibly put an end to it.

Now that the above groundwork has been explained, allow me to continue with the information that has only recently been brought to light, regarding lopped ears on Continental Giants. This began in the spring of 2020. (Of course, it would be 2020, the year of every-kind-of-crazy going hay-wire that could be imagined.) Several breeders noticed a problem that presented with ear mites. This was not the typical case of mites, however. Normally, while ear mites are no fun to deal with, they can easily and successfully be dealt with and eradicated. These cases were not like that, at all. The breeders would see the mites, do the typical cleaning and treating, the mites would be gone – and then within 2 to 3 days, the infestation would be right back to the point of severity, as if nothing had been done to begin with. No matter treatment was used, they simply would not go away! Revolution does not work. Advantage does not work. Ivermec does not work. You are welcome to argue the point that those treatments did or do work all you wish to argue about it, but unless you have directly dealt with this exact scenario – do yourself a favor - and do not kid yourself. These little bad-boys absolutely would not go away. They were being questioned as being a new strain of ear mites, somewhat like a 'super-bug' that had mutated and become resistant to everything on the market. As luck would have it though, several others began talking about having the same problem.

That is when exact details and symptoms started being listed out, bloodlines began being traced, and other rabbit breeds - which were exposed- were being monitored as well. With that information at hand, it became clear that the problem only presented in Conti with a lopped ear. This mostly seemed to effect babies, but definitely not in all cases. The bunny would display head shaking, often would have scratch marks on the ear from scratching, the fur would be dull and lifeless, and weight loss became very noticeable as well. Additionally, one person involved in the original case, while cleaning and treating for the mite infestation, had also noticed a rancid, foul odor. That information was then passed along, and in almost all of the cases, the breeder would be able to smell the odor, even in non-parasitic filled ears, by actually putting their nose down to the opening of the ear canal and breathing in deeply. Right! Not very pleasant, but, when there is a mystery going on, no stone can be left unturned.

During this investigative period of time, other things were also noted. Some breeders had taken their lop-eared Conti to their vet, where an ear exam would be done. The results of that exam, repeatedly, were that "everything looked ok." From there, other questions came into play, such as wondering if this was an entirely different type of mite, or maybe a completely new parasite altogether. Then came the realization that other breeds of rabbits, which were housed right next to the heavily infested Conti, were not being affected at all; not in one single instance did a different breed get the mites. These super-bugs were, indeed, appearing to only be affecting the Conti. I know what you surely are thinking, "that's crazy!" That is exactly what my thoughts were, anyway. Yet, in each situation, not one breeder had experienced the problem spreading to any of their other rabbits – only the Conti. Additionally, the more that two and two were added together, it appeared to be mainly involving one or two particular bloodlines. That theory, however, was short lived and easily laid to rest. But the fact remained, why only the Continentals? Why were the Flemish, French, Polish, Angoras, English, Hollands, or other various breeds of rabbits not getting these mites? It made no sense at all. It wasn't until about two weeks later, when all of the pieces were put together, that the puzzle began taking shape.

As more cases were brought to light, I began working with a lady who is also a Vet-Management Consultant with approximately 10-years of Vet-Med ER/Specialty experience, Amanda Zachrich. With her assistance, along with numerous tests and procedures provided by an unnamed Exotic Veterinary Hospital which, according to Amanda, was previously featured on the show "Animal ER, National Geographic Top Notch Exotic Doctors," that some answers began rolling in.

Please make certain that you, the reader, completely and fully understand the diagnosis of this, as I am told by Amanda, cannot be done by a routine ear exam, by a general or exotic vet. The only way to absolutely and properly diagnose this is by *Sedated Aural Exam with Video Otoscope*. Otherwise, this condition will likely be misdiagnosed as Idiopathic Head Tremors or Subclinical E-Cuniculi Infection. Again, let me say it loudly, so the back row doesn't miss this: the way to diagnose this correctly is by the above mentioned *sedated exam with video otoscope, and you will most likely need an exotic vet for this.

The test results reported from the above noted exam: Entropion (congenital eyelid abnormality), Stenotic Canals in both ears, and in the lopped ear, the eardrum had ruptured along with a raging bacterial infection in the middle ear, without the presence of mites. The non-lopped ear was also found to be inflamed. None of which was able to be seen with a normal, routine exam or testing. Additionally, E-Cuniculi was not present.

Now, buckle your seat belts folks, because this is where we are going to get real! Here is the bottom line, and for the record, the Exotic Vets involved agree on the probability of cause. Continental Giants, believed to have been created with the involvement of crossing a Flemish Giant to a French Lop, which was created by crossing a Flemish to an English Lop. This practice is still continued by many breeders in many countries, especially with the German Greys (aka German Giants, which is essentially a Continental Giant) and this is exactly what, at this point, appears to be the cause of this entire situation because the lop-eared breeds are genetically predisposed to external ear canal bacterial infections; this is due to the narrowed and obstructed shape of the canal, resulting from the ears bending into the lopped position.

If you do your homework and look up the anatomical structure of French Lop breed rabbits' heads and compare that to the structure of a Flemish Giant heads, the difference is sobering. Paying particular attention to the ear, notice the ear shape and the narrowed, obstructed ear canals of the lop breeds. They are, indeed, very narrow and small. That is not the case with a Flemish. We know the Conti get their ear-base from the Flemish, which is what causes the ear to stand erect. But consider this: What would the genetic outcome be if you take those erect, large, wide ears and set them on top of tiny little ear canals? If you guessed a loss of base strength, you guessed correctly! Now, add to that the fact that any object that is narrow and small is hard to access. If you cannot access it, you cannot thoroughly clean it, and that also means that you have no idea what kind of shape the inner ear and eardrum are in. Then, take one more step here and consider the fact that common sense will tell you that large, tall, wide cup-shaped ears which are open are going to 'catch' more debris and bacteria. It is unavoidable! Next, add natural gravity to that mix. What happens to anything that is standing erect and has something that gets 'caught', regardless of how minuscule it may be, by a wide, cup shaped object? Yep! All of that gunk is going down … straight into that tiny little already obstructed ear canal, which is already predisposed to bacterial infection, and that cannot be clearly seen or cleaned out. Bingo!! You end up with a wild fire that quickly gets out of control. From here, I'm sure you can imagine how fast an ugly infection could become chronic; and if that is not bad enough, ask yourself – what attracts parasites? The answer, of course, is places that are wet, damp, dark, and have an odor. Now you're seeing the point. The mites are drawn and burrow very deeply into the ear, down past those really small ear canals, into the ear drums, where you and your vet are unable to see easily or properly clean out. Those mites then begin to multiple, and boom! You have a raging infection and trapped mites. As the mites continue multiplying, that is when they become visible and obviously, that is when owners and vets would begin treatment. The mites would appear to go away, for a short time. But, because they were never entirely eradicated to begin with, they just continue multiplying and returning visibly.

Do I have your attention yet? Well, don't stop reading now, because there is still more to learn, here. As if all of this information is not enough of a nightmare, lets next consider what we already know is a large problem with Continental babies and young juniors. Even though most breeders will not openly admit it, it is very common for babies to die of what is 'guessed' as being or often referred to as "Failure to Thrive". You know the ones; they seem ok one minute, yet when you turn around, without warning, symptom, or signs, they are found dead. Some breeders have suspected some sort of a neurological abnormality as being the cause. However, it could be very possible that this entire train-wreck is caused by this very problem – stenotic canals which cause raging infections. How could that be? Easily; the infection spreads and attaches to the skull and then it becomes systemic, affecting the brain, as well as possibly the central nervous system, and into the organs, including but not limited to the gastrointestinal tract. When this happens, what would you expect to see happen? If you are thinking head shaking, scratching, lopped ears, with weight loss, poor fur condition, and over-all listlessness which may or may not include a bloated stomach, heart disease, kidney disease, liver disease, or any other number of internal damages, you guess correctly. Additionally, if that bunny is just a baby, it is equally possible that such a condition could occur and kill, without warning.

So, what can be done about all of this? Well, first of all, a correct diagnosis needs to be made. Beyond that though, don't throw in the towel because there is hope. A suggested vet treatment involved thorough flushing of the ear with Enrofloxacin and Triz cleaner with antibiotic treatment, for one month, with either Baytril,

Chloramphenicol, PenG / Bicillin. The chosen course of action, in this case, was to avoid oral meds due to the susceptibility of gut problems occurring. Therefore, PenG would be given at a rate of one injection per day, for 7 days, followed by injections every other day for the remaining 3 weeks, with an additional antibiotic being used in conjunction, on alternating days, in case the bacteria could be resistant and would require more than the typical treatment. Gabapentin and Metacam were also discussed. Furthermore, after the antibiotics have been given, the suggestion was to then follow up with Ivermec, as an ear drop, because -as we had previously discovered – Revolution and Advantage are not strong enough to do the job needed, and on the basis that once the infection was cleared up, the Ivermec would then be able to get down deeply enough into the canal so that it could properly do its job of eradicating the mites. Note here, it's not just one product that fixed the problem. It required a combination of meds to do the job.

For those who may not have the luxury of access to an exotic vet, and who fully understand the factors of self-treating being by done entirely of their own accord, and at their own risk, here are some options that have already proven to be effective. First, do your very best to determine the cause and make sure that you are treating properly. If you then choose to then pursue this, the course of action for mites, if present, is with an oil-based solution; Mineral Oil or even good old-fashioned Veggie Oil have done a good job. The goal is to remove as much mite-gunk as possible. Then flush the ear out with the oil solution. Do not use water! Doing this will definitely set up and infection, or make a current one even worse. Next, begin dosing with Pen-G, and if possible, a 2nd brand of antibiotic, such as Baytril. The above referenced exotic vets' have reported that mycin-based meds have proven to be ineffective for mite issues, by the way. Treat for no less than 21 days. Once the ears appear to be mite-free, use Ivermec AS an ear drop. Count out 1 drop per body pound (ie: 10 drops for 10lbs) and divide that amount in half. Place half of those drops into one ear and the other half into the other ear; place the drops as best you can so that they will get down into the ear canal, and then one week later, repeat the process. It is additionally suggested that you also sanitize all surfaces that your rabbit is in. Once you have cleaned, you can then also spray the areas with "Good Night Away Spray". This is available at Farm Supply type stores, and is actually used for killing bed-bugs. Make absolutely certain that all surfaces are completely dry before allowing your rabbit to return to the area.

One more time, let me reiterate: I am not a vet. I do suggest you work with an exotic vet. If you do choose to use any suggestions for any reasons, you are doing so at your own risk! Any and all of the information that I offer here, or anywhere else, at any time, is strictly for informational purposes based on things that have been done either by myself or others (permission given to note it) which has provided positive outcomes.

Otherwise, what you choose to do with this information is your own decision and I am in no way liable for your actions.

Finally, don't shoot the messenger – but – do you remember in the last chapter when Malocclusion was discussed? Just to back up that information, after reading this chapter, can you see the relativity between the two issues? By breeding the blocky headed French Lop with the longer head of the European style Conti or Flemish Giant, not only are stenotic canals likely causing congenital abnormalities, it is also very possibly the exact same reason that the malocclusion has also become more predominant in Continentals. To put it simply, the jaw structures do not line up correctly, causing the teeth to be misaligned and over-grown.

SIX
Feet

Another prevalent problem with a lot of Giant bunnies, Conti included, is that they tend to be prone to sore hocks, aka Pododermatitis. Count yourself blessed if you have not had to deal with this factor. While it can usually be treated effectively, it is no fun for you or for your furry friend.

Sore hocks are most commonly caused from your giant rabbit being on a harsh or abrasive surface, especially an enclosure with wire flooring. Considering that rabbits are on their feet for the largest part of their lives, and adding the size and weight of a Conti's body being pressed down onto those wires, well, you're looking at a disaster waiting to get started. If your Conti's feet are not heavily padded with fur, that also adds to their susceptibility of developing these awful, raw, sore spots on their feet.

Having a wire, or otherwise harsh flooring is not the only cause for this condition, however. It can also be caused by the floor surface being damp or wet – most often due to bedding being soaked from urine or feces, which causes the fur and skin on the pads of their feet to break down and become weaker. The next most common problem is when your rabbit is often stressed and / or tends to stomp their hind feet a lot. Repetitive stomping can actually cause trauma to the feet, resulting in the pads of their feet then weakening and breaking down. Long toenails are another factor, as they prevent your rabbit from being able to stand and walk properly. When this happens, they put all of their weight on a certain area of the feet, often the heels, and because their body is not being upheld and supported correctly, the over-and-improperly used portion of the feet wear down. This causes the skin to then break down and the sores develop due to that. Arthritis will also play its part, causing the same results as the long toenails cause, however, this is more common in older giants. Injuries, especially those which involve the toes, feet, leg, hip, or spine could even be the culprit. It is also believed by many breeders that sore hocks and other abscesses are in some way hereditary in the means that some lines may tend to be more prone to developing these issues than others. Personally, I have seen this type of reoccurrence, although I cannot say that it has been proven, scientifically, to be factual. In the cases I have witnessed, however, the actual cause seems to be weak bone, combined with poorly padded feet. If you also find a correlation is the problem being predominately with one particular line you work with, then I would suggest culling the entire line that you have (soft or hard) from your breeding program to remove the problem in future litters.

If your bunny develops sores on his feet, it is important to discover the cause. If you do not, the condition will continue reoccurring, and you will end up with a nightmare on your hands, as this condition can and does actually cause bacterial infections, which can spread thru the bloodstream and even infect the bone. Once this begins, unless you are one of the select few who realize that there is such a deep problem going on, the chances are high that your rabbit will eventually die from, or need to be euthanized because of the infection becoming septic and untreatable. By the way, any recurring issue with sore hocks, especially if the condition progresses into an abscess, is your first indicator that you do, in fact, have a very serious problem on your hands.

So, how do you know if your bunny has sore hocks? Easy! If you see your giant pal leaning to one side, favoring one area of a foot, or spending time hunched up in one spot? You go back to the very basics. Do not wait. Take him out of his enclosure immediately and do a basic health exam. This is always your first step, to visually and physically feel the entire rabbit from head to toe, regardless of what you suspect as being the problem at hand. Beyond that though, if you notice the skin on any foot is inflamed, red, swollen, or obviously raw and bleeding, or if you see any type of a callus or blister on any foot, then you are most likely dealing with sore hocks.

What do you do if there is evidence, noted above, of this problem? Well, you have two choices, initially. You can attempt to treat on your own, or you can call an Exotic Vet for advice and treatment. Obviously, if you choose the latter, your Vet will exam the feet and other areas and will then give you their assessment, followed by their suggest course of treatment. This could include topical ointments and possibly oral or injective antibiotics, and depending on the severity of the situation at hand, he may also offer something for pain relief.

If you decide to treat on your own, you will need to pull out your handy emergency kit, which hopefully you already have well-stocked with a wide variety of items. For this, you will specifically want to have topical ointments. The most commonly used are just basic over-the-counter items are Neosporin, Bag Balm, and/or Preparation H. My preference, however, is Colloidal Silver (Silver Sulfadiazine) – which I have found, countless times, to be an amazing go-to for dozens of issues. Others' also swear on using Manuka Honey, which can also be combined or mixed with any of the above items, or used alone. Then, depending on the presence and severity of infection, you may also need to offer an antibiotic. Regardless of what the antibiotic is used for, I always suggest and highly recommend the use of an injectable form for the simple fact that every single thing that you put into your rabbits GI Tract can quickly cause a gut problem which will lead to a whole other mess that you do not want to have to deal with, if there is any way at all in preventing it from happening. Remember here, too, that your rabbit is already stressed out from being in pain and not being able to properly use his feet, so any other added stressor is only going to complicate matters. Additionally, injectable forms do tend to work faster than oral forms. Many owners choose to use Pen-G as their go to or form of antibiotic. Again, unless abscesses are involved, my preference is different for the reason that Pen-G is a very aggressive type of medication, which is not always required to get the job done. With that said, if there are no abscesses present, I use LA-200, which is a broad-spectrum antibiotic. Additionally, I know others who prefer the sulfa-based options, such as Tetracycline. Baytril is another choice, however, I find that works best on issues which involve mucous membranes and respiratory system. Otherwise, as I have repeated throughout this book, I am not offering you dosage amounts because I am not a Vet and am not willing to take the responsibility of that risk; you can find dosage information in a vast number of places on the internet, if you need that. For added measure, you can also spray the infect foot with Betadine. This, as well as most other supplies, can be found at your local Farm Supply Stores, or ordered online.

In addition to the medication options, I also suggest, if you can manage to do so, that you wrap the infected feet. Begin by covering the area in a couple layers of gauze pads, then securely bind that to the foot with self-adhesive sports-wrap. Yes, before you ask, all rabbits hate having their feet wrapped and they will do everything they can to yank that off. There is a trick to getting it to stay in place though (at least for a little while). To do so, you will need to place the gauze and wrap it once or twice, just around the area of gauze, then using an "X" pattern – continue to secure the tape around the foot and leg. Make sure that you are not wrapping it too tightly, or too loosely, and do not cover the ankle in a manner that prohibits flexible movement. Additionally, don't beat yourself up if your bunny has this pulled the wrapping off in an hour. It takes practice to get the dressing and pressure correct, and in a way that it will stay in place, at least for several hours or even until time for the next treatment and dressing-change. The point of doing this, even when the bunny pulls it off, is the fact that any amount of time that you can keep that area clean, the better and faster it will heal.

From this point on, you will also need to do a deep and thorough cleaning and sanitation of the enclosure; particularly pay attention to the floor and bedding. Make certain that the flooring is *sanitized with *disinfectant, *clean, and *dry! If this is not done, you are only spinning circles and wasting time in treating because the problem will just continue coming back – if it goes away at all. Also, make sure that you soften the flooring. This means get the bunny off the wire, if he is on wire. If all you have is wire enclosures, you can still cover that wire with something. The most common things for covering wire is to cover the floor with a heavy rubber mat, or even a thick piece of carpet will work. Then, cover that area with soft bedding (referring back to an earlier chapter), I recommend using Aspen Shavings. Others prefer straw or hay. The reason I don't recommend either is because straw is hard and stiff, and they will eat straw and hay; if they are using the bedding as a toilet (which is highly likely), and they absolutely eat, or at least nibble on that. If that happens (which it will) what you likely will end up with is a parasitic problem. Obviously, the goal in all of this is to prevent and treat problems – not create new ones.   Otherwise, if your bunny as free-roam of your home and you notice issues with sore hocks, I would lean towards the problem being genetic, such as the culprit, at least in part, being weak bone and / or poorly padded feet.

Lastly, I will briefly note that if you are noticing a problem with recurring abscesses, don't try to continually fight this on your own. Call your Exotic Vet and make an appointment because there is likely a much deeper problem going on. For instance, if a prior infection was severe, it could have become systematically spread, causing the entire immune system to get messed up. Only a Vet can make that judgment call, and if that call is made, a very aggressive treatment will be required – if it is possible to save the bunny beyond that point.

SEVEN
Brains, Organs, and Bones

Neurological issues in rabbits may seem a little far-fetched to some, but they exist, and moreso than you may realize. Continental Giants are, by no means, immune to these issues. So, while we are focusing on the Conti, a lot of the information in this book may also be very prevalent with other breeds, too.

So, how do you know you might be dealing with a neurological problem? Some of the most common symptoms will include wry neck (tilted head), paralysis, behavioral changes, tremors, and seizures. There are various causes for these symptoms. What may come as a surprise, however, is that also most commonly, the conditions are often due to infections or trauma. The only way to be certain of what is going on though is by exotic vet exams, which may include but are not limited to x-rays, blood, bacterial, and other culture testing, physical exam and, of course, neurological exams.

One of the most commonly seen problems is E-Cuniculi and Pasteurella, with both caused by infection, resulting from or involving mite infestation. The symptoms of Pasteurella include sneezing, the presence of mucous around the nose and eyes, and a rattling sound in lungs. With E-Cuniculi, the symptoms include behavior changes, rolling or having seizures, incontinence, and head tilt. Fenbendazole is a common medication for treatment, and there is some talk of favorable response when the rabbit has been given the same types of medications that humans use for motion sickness, however, more information on this is not yet known.

If infection is present it will often present as a thick yellow pus in the middle or inner ear, and that infection is on one side, the head will tilt down on the affected side. The skull may also show soft tissue density and the ear drum may rupture as well. Inflammation is also common. In many cases, the head tilt cannot be reversed, but it can sometimes be kept from getting worse when treated with antibiotics. Baytril and Ciprofloxacin are commonly successful for treatment. If treatment is effective, there should be indication of that within one week. Although the antibiotic is typically prescribed for two weeks. It is important to follow the instruction for the full length of time if told to give for two weeks. In addition to antibiotic treatment, the affected ear should also be cleaned and flushed. A commonly suggested solution for flushing the ear is a mixture of 0.5% Enrofloxacin and 1% Silver Sulfadiazine (Baytril Otic).

Other, less common causes of neurological issues with rabbits include hypoxia, metastatic tumors, bacterial encephalitis, listeria, epilepsy, and meningitis. In all of these cases, diagnosis and treatment can be accurately assessed under the guidance and assistance of a knowledgeable, experienced exotic vet. Because of these being less common, and for the risks of someone 'taking a guess', rather than having a complete and accurate diagnosis, medications and treatments are not going to be added here.

Nerve Damage is another issue that should be checked out. This is often difficult to determine because the symptoms are often the same as other neurologically based disorders. Some are caused by exposure to parasites and infections, others are possibly caused by congenital abnormalities (hereditary), injury, environment, and nutrition. Any type of nerve damage is going to affect the nervous system of your rabbit and will likely be referred to as a neurological disorder as well. Again, the only way to know what you truly are dealing with is by visiting your vet, who will do physical and neurological exams, blood and other serum-based labs, and imagery tests. Various types of treatments may be offered, however, there is no 'one size fits all' standardized option, and unfortunately, if your bunny's health continues to decline, euthanasia may be suggested.

Heart disease is another avenue that cannot be ignored. Some of the symptoms include lethargy, weakness, reduced appetite with sudden weight changes, labored breathing, and bloating may also occur as liver and GI Stasis can display as a secondary type of indicator of the heart not functioning normally. While this cannot be cured, medication and other changes of lifestyle may help alleviate the conditions. A healthy, normal heart rate for a rabbit is within the range of 140 to 180 beats per minute. When he becomes anxious or upset, that can raise to as high as about 300 beats per minute, and yes, just the trip to the Vet's office can be enough to push those numbers up, making it harder for diagnosis to be made without further testing.

Liver disease, more correctly called Hepatic Steatosis, can be due to having an excessive amount of fat in the liver cells. This is often caused by a diet that is too high in carbs, resulting in the rabbit to be unable to process the excess as needed and ends up causing cellular and toxic wastes in the blood. There will be a loss of appetite, often caused by stress, pain, dental problems, and quite the list of other issues. Additionally, if the liver is involved, you may or may not also notices signs of jaundice, as you would with a human, by the whites of the eyes becoming a yellowish color. A liver enzyme test would be required to be fully diagnose and evaluate the condition.

The very beginning of what holds a rabbits' structure is their bones, and the one thing that may surprise you is that if you research this, you will find a large variety of answers to 'how many bones does a rabbit have?' In some cases, the informant only reported a rabbit having 23 types of bones. In other locations, it is reported that the number is from 206 up to 381 (baby) or 361 (adult). There doesn't seem to be one solid concise number being repeated. Personally, I have never physically sat down and attempted to count the amount of bones in a rabbit – and I am not going to. So, while it was worth mentioning for this section, this author is choosing to let the subject rest with the response of 'an exact number is not known, personally.' Regardless however, the number of bones isn't the reason for this information, so, we will just hop right along.

What we do know is that Continental Giants have larger bones than smaller breeds, and of course common sense tells us that, due to the mere size of them. To support their body and weight, those bones must be strong and healthy. This begins with the cellular structure and carries through into all of the other physically structural parts of the animal. What happens though, if a Conti ends up with fine, thin, or weak bones? Well, obviously, they would be more prone to fractures and breaks. The severity and location of any such injury would be what determines the result. For example, a rabbit can break a toe and live, but if the spine is broken, that would not be the case. Additionally, depending on the severity and location of the break, there are several options of treatment. This can range from immobilization, splinting or casting, to surgical insertion of pins to rejoin the bones, and possibly even amputation. In most of these cases, the rabbit can go on to have a good life. As previously mentioned, if it is the spine, surgery is not usually an option, and at that time, it is commonly suggested to end the bunny's suffering and opt for euthanasia.

EIGHT
Digestive Disorders

If you know anything about Continental Giant rabbits at all, you will already have an understanding for the fact that these magnificent creatures are prone to gut problems. To begin with, all rabbits have sensitive digestive systems, but when you double, triple, or quadruple the size of the animal, as would be the case when comparing, let's say, a Netherland Dwarf or Polish, to the Conti, common sense should be the first clue of noticing that the problems with that sensitivity is also going to increase and then it gets even more complicated due to the amount of free-range of space, which is seen more commonly with these gentle giants, as it allows more options for their curiously wondering mouths to discover, plus the fact that just because it's not a plant, doesn't mean they won't attempt to eat it; they will chew pretty much anything that they can get their teeth around, and if they can chew it, they will swallow it.

When our furry friends are behaving and eating what they are supposed to have, the digestive system works fine usually. But if you add in fibrous materials and other indigestible items, well, all sort of chaos can get started. Furthermore, keeping your bunny on a well-balanced diet is vital for his life. I will offer more detail on nutrition in a later chapter though.

The first issue we will look into is GI Stasis. This can become fatal if not caught and dealt with quickly enough. This, by the way, also refers to the commonly known "wool block". The cause of Stasis is due to the inability to process what has been eaten, be it ingested fur, fibers from stuffed animals, blankets, rugs, carpet, and a long list of other things that has no business being in the GI tract to begin with. I will also note here that some people think that there is no harm done in giving their bunny such items as toys. For some that may work out, but I will say that I never suggest allowing such a thing because of the simple rule of 'when in doubt, throw it out'. In other words, if you know that there is even a small chance that offering such things to your pet could cause deadly results, why in the world would you choose to give it to them. To each their own, however, common sense tells me that even if you are lucky some of the time, eventually, that luck will run out and you'll be faced with paying the piper. Others may argue, too, that they offer preventatives, such as the papaya tablets, to counter-act such problems. However, again, my reply to that is always the same; if you were more selective in not allowing such risks to start with, there wouldn't be a problem to be concerned with. As it is, licking and ingesting their fur is plenty enough reason to be mindful, so what gainful purpose is there in choosing to promote further risks. If you are bound and determined to do so though, good luck and I wish you and your pal the best. If you find that you do have a problem though, the quickest acting aid that I have found has been Chewable Papaya Enzyme Tablets which can be found in nearly any vitamin section of most stores which carry such items. Rabbits cannot overdose on papaya, so you're good. Some rabbits will eat these tablets as they are, others will not. If Stasis is in full blown effect, you my notice strands of hair in the poop, or they may completely be constipated, and if the bunny has stopped eating, you then may need to pulverize some of the tablets into powder (crush them between two spoons) and mix into a small amount of room temperature water to syringe feed it, or add the powdered tablets into their water – if they are still eating and drinking normally.

Next, gut problems arise from bacteria building up in the gut and intestines. This can begin by anything that shocks or otherwise throws the flora in their gut into either over drive, or non-functioning status. In other words, they will either end up with diarrhea or constipation. In either case, a bloated stomach is common. Other indicators will be lethargy, behavioral changes, and the appetite will decrease, resulting with them not eating or drinking. Also, you may or may not notice mucous in the poop – without the presence of a foul or unusual odor. This is a common issue with younger rabbits, from the time they begin eating up until they reach about 4 months of age.

I am going to further note here, when it comes to the above situation – known as Enteritis – I have spent two years researching just this topic alone. During my research, I conducted tests and trials, I read everything I could get my hands on, watched videos, spoke to general vets, exotic vets, vet techs, and spoke to countless-hundreds of breeders of various types of rabbits. I created flow charts and measured results very carefully on every variety and form of "cure" that I could come up with. I even charted liter size, exact feed increments, space allotted for physical activity, and noted if there were any differences in the reactions of the bucks vs does and testing for Flemish giant vs Continental giant, plus I created a public blog with 'some' of that information, which can still be found on my personal rabbitry website. Without fail, failure was to be found in every direction when Conti were involved and only twice did a litter of Flemish giants ever display the condition. Furthermore, I continued also logging which bloodlines were involved, to check for specific congenital conditions, only to find that it effected all Conti lines, with both imported and US-lineage. In every case, not one single 'cure' found provided consistent results, other than death. When I say here that there was not one stone that I left unturned – you can take that to the bank! And it was not until we, my husband and I, created a recipe that I named and is known as "Cel-Gin" had one single baby ever survived the problem. Additionally, from that recipe, I created fast-fix recipes as well as longer, more complex recipes. Then, without fail, every single baby that I treated survived! And not only did it survive, it suffered no stunted growth or other long-term problem due to the fact that it was "a bloat survivor"; and best of all, every item used in these recipes are natural foods. What does that mean? It means that it is not causing further damage or risk of further interference with the GI System either during or after treatment. I then tested and tested and tested these recipes for one year before I ever spoke a word to a single person about it, and again – pay attention here folks – Not. One. Baby. Died. and Not. One. Baby. Had. A. Single. Adverse. Reaction. From. It. In every single case, the baby pulled through with flying colors, and did so within 4 to 48 hours of treatments. After that year of full success, I began telling others and they began using it. In every single case that the problem was truly Enteritis – every person, to the best of my knowledge, had the same results that I have had: 100% Survival with no adverse side effects or reactions. So, you decide... if you want to continue using whatever other methods you came up with – knock yourself out. But there is absolutely no convincing me, for any reason, that there is not one single solitary thing in existence for this problem that can or will beat the results that the Cel-Gin has proven, time and time again, to provide. I'm not saying this either, to make money or in attempt to sell you a product. I have freely given away this recipe to anyone who asks, and have done so for a couple years. My only concern is to help the rabbits, by helping you to help them. Just for the record here, because this world is full of crazy, sue-happy, trouble-makers, drama-queens, and other such 'fine folks', I also am reminding you of my disclaimer that I am not a vet. I am not telling you to, or not to, use any information that I am or have offered, and any form of action that you take or choose to use is entirely of your own free will. I am in no way, shape, or form liable for any results received.

Next, let's take a quick look at what contributes to gut mobility issues. Plain and simple, the most common and over-looked thing is stress. Conti are notorious for being extremely prone to stress. Things that many may not even consider is enough to cause a stressful reaction from this breed. Why this breed is more susceptible than other breeds, in all honesty, I have no idea. However, it is very true! Some of the triggers include but are not limited to:

- changing types of feed or content in feed
- adding new foods to diet

- changing location
- separation from mom and/or litter-mates
- unusual sounds
- loud or startling sounds
- unfamiliar animals – via sight, sound, or scent
- the presence of unfamiliar people
- a change in water
- adding or removing items from their enclosure-environment,
- parasites
- infections and other health-related issues, such as dental and ear problems
- sudden changes in temperatures
- transportation to or from any location, especially -but not limited to long distances

In other words, pretty much anything and everything can become stressful to Conti. While that seems like a heavy load to bare, here is your next tip. Once the babies are past 12 weeks of age, these problems become less of a threat. Then, by the time they reach 16+ weeks of age, the problem pretty much disappears. It is possible for older bunnies to run into some issues with these problems, however, what I am saying is that the older they get, the less likely they are to have a problem. This is because as they get older, the immune systems strengthen, as does their exposure rates and as that occurs, the better mentally and emotionally they are to withstand such factors. This is exactly why it is so vital that any and all breeders stop pushing 8-10week old babies out of their hands. Buyers, take note here as well; if any breeder tries to demand that you take a baby that is 10 weeks old or younger – Walk. Away. Furthermore, buyers, do not be asking, let alone begging, for any breeder to let you pick your baby up before it is 12 weeks old. Ideally, even the 12-week old babies need to be kept with the breeder longer. I've heard all of the excuses in the book! Not one single one of them justifies that fact of why a breeder cannot hold onto a baby for an extra couple of weeks. If the mom is picking on the baby and it must be separated – then do so, but keep it in your care. The same applies if its problems with litter-mates picking on each other. Otherwise, if you – the breeder – does not have the space or the financial means to hold those babies that you created, then you should not be creating them until you do have the financial means and space. If that upsets you, well, I'm not sorry. It is the truth and it needs to be said – and everyone needs to understand it. If you are not going to take responsibility for what you created, you should not be creating it. Likewise, buyers, if transport availability is your reason for pushing a baby to be released to you early – wait for the next run; they happen all the time, all over the nation. If your concern is wanting the rabbit to bond with you, age is not your concern. The care, time, and attention that you provide once it is in your hands is all there needs to be in order for that bonding to occur. Even mature senior aged Conti can and will bond with you when given the proper time to do so.

Otherwise, for those reading this who think they know better and all of the above is just words spoken to fill a page; well, go on, knock yourself out! But when you run into problems, and you will – at some point, it WILL come back to bite you, and it will bite you hard when it does - and your rabbit gets sick and / or ends up dead – don't cry about it – because you caused it to happen. Also, don't then be upset and start trashing others for what you caused to begin with. Sorry… but not sorry.

NINE
Nutrition

There are lots of people out there who will tell you who-only-even-knows-what when it comes to the amount of food that a rabbit needs daily, also. That doesn't help matters much. Actually, it can even complicate things – depending on who you are listening to. I am not here to correct, debate, or rectify any of the above. So, if you are one that requires a measured amount, sorry, but I'm not one to tell you that. What I will say is that my personal rule of thumb is this:

rabbits don't eat like humans – consuming food just because it is sitting there and they are bored. They eat when they are hungry, although they might over-eat if allowed to do so, especially if what they are eating is one of their favorite things to nibble on. So, I give each rabbit the number of pellets that they typically will eat 3/4ths of in one 10-minute setting. This leaves a small amount in the bowl, in which they can snack on if needed. Otherwise, they get greens and hay, with the occasional treat of fruit. It is important here to also note that if your rabbit is more physically active, they will eat more because they are burning more calories from that added activity. Likewise, those big funny couch-potato bunnies will need less, because they lack the extra physical activity.

In regard specifically to the greens, while other breeds of rabbits seem to do well with or without receiving their fair share of greens, when it comes to Conti, that isn't so much the case. With these amazing big bunnies, it is pretty easy to see which ones get fed the greens and which ones do not. The ones who do, thrive! They tend to be almost $1/4^{th}$ larger or more, than the ones who do not get them. Also, I should note here that by 'greens', I mean veggies and plants, such as plantain, dandelion, and other naturally growing 'weeds' that they love. Furthermore, if you are curious about what specifically is or is not safe for them, a list has been provided in the book, *Continental Giant Rabbits, Advanced Tips for care, feeding, housing, and health*.

Next, I want to briefly discuss hay. So, a whole lot of people may disagree here; but I am going to say it. Not every rabbit even likes hay. Yep! It's the truth. Some of them are allergic to it, or the dust in it, perhaps; causing them to sneeze every time you give it to them. This is no joke! I've watched it happen. But too, there are others who love one type of hay and refuse all others. The bottom line is that they can certainly be picky eaters. My point in saying all of this is to say that 'old wives' tale' of rabbit requiring hay to live... yeah, that is as false as the day is long. If they required it to live, the wild ones would be hard pressed for survival during winter months and the domestic rabbits who refuse it, well, they would be doomed from the get-go. Now, this also does not mean that I am telling you not to give it to your rabbits. That is not at all what I am saying. Rather, what I am saying, is that while I agree that they should have it, it is also true that their world will not end without it. The primary purpose of hay, additionally, is to provide a higher fiber content in their diets and to help them keep their teeth in good condition. Fortunately, there are also several other ways to provide the same benefits.

Beet Pulp, for instance, is an excellent source of fiber. You can get it at Farm Supply type stores that carry horse feed. There are usually a couple options in regard to the size of bag you get. Just make sure that you get the type which is shredded and has no added molasses or sugar. There is no need at all to soak it before feeding. In fact, not soaking it doubles the benefit, as that will also cover the need of assisting in dental conditioning - which would otherwise be received in the hay. All you need to do is give them one pinch, or the size of a teaspoon, of the shredded beet pulp, every other day. Just mix it into their pellets, or set it on top of the pellets, as a 'top-dress'. Most rabbits love it and will love you for it.

If you are fortunate enough to have a hay-loving bunny, in case you don't already know, yes - there are different types of hay for a reason. Alfalfa has the highest carb content of the types of hay. It is suggested that this only be given to pregnant and nursing does and babies which have not yet been weaned. The reason is simple; it will help keep their metabolism rates up, so they will be able to gain and maintain a healthier weight during such active stages of life. As those babies begin moving and are weaned, you may wish to them switch them over to Timothy / Alfalfa mix hay, and then either keep them on that, or after they become senior aged, then switch them over to pure Timothy, Timothy / Orchard Grass, or another type of hay. Doing so will prevent them from gaining too much weight, which likely would occur if they were to continue eating pure Alfalfa. Additionally, the reason you don't want a 'fat bunny' is because fat is unhealthy! It causes fatty liver disease, and increases other problems in vital organs, plus it can and will prevent does from becoming pregnant.

Now, the reason why it is a good idea to allow your Conti to have the occasional fruit is because fruits are loaded with vitamins. Just as it is with humans and any other species of animals, without the proper vitamin content, the body begins lacking in one or more areas. Vitamin C, as we all know, boosts the immune system. Therefore, giving your furry friend a little apple will help to keep their Vitamin C levels in good proportion, plus it will boost fiber. As it is with carrots, however, apples are also high in natural sugars, so always remember to only give moderate amounts. Bunnies love bananas; they are loaded with potassium. Blueberries are an excellent source of antioxidants. Papaya is full of calcium, folic acid, vitamin c, fiber, and carotenoids, plus this will be your saving-grace if your fuzzy pal gets wool-block because it will quickly dissolve any fibers in the gut and intestinal track. Raisins are a good source of iron and fiber, too, just be careful with the high calories and sugar involved with them. Next, Strawberries and Raspberries are great for vitamin c, folic acid, and zinc. Buy organic though, because these magnificent sweets are nearly impossible to wash very well, and are typically heavily sprayed with pesticides.

As it is with all of life, remember that too much of a good thing can easily go bad. This is the very thing that makes the term "balanced meal" meaningful. Think about it for a moment. If you were to offer a child an unlimited amount of sweet sugary treats every day, how many green veggies do you think that child would willingly eat? Right! Not many, if any at all. The same would apply with rabbits, and it would carry over into other things, such as hay verses pellets. If you offered huge amounts of their favorite hay, how many pellets do you think they would be willing to eat? See how that works? Just like you probably were taught as a youngster; dinner first, and then dessert. It really is not very complicated, once you get the basic idea of how body's function. The reason all of this matter is because the physical body needs more than just one or two things to survive; and in order to really thrive, their needs to a balanced amount of all the nutrients required throughout the entire body.

TEN
Reproduction

One of the most common comments heard in conversations between rabbit breeders is "who-ever said they breed like rabbits clearly has never tried to breed rabbits." That little tidbit of truth echo's loudly when you're talking about Continental Giants. There are several issues that could be hindering your hopes of breeding the pair you are wanting to produce offspring from.

In the same way that humans are picky about who they choose to take as a mate, the truth is, Conti can be and often are equally as picky. Maybe it's a scent issue, or maybe they just know what they like. But if you have a specific pair that you are wanting not breed, the chances may be fairly high that you have experienced just how difficult making it happen can actually be. In fact, quite a few things come into play when it comes to breeding issues. Among the most common problems, there is stress, weather, age, lighting, weight, ventilation, and just plain stubbornness or dislike.

Weather, lighting, and ventilation are easily fixed. After all, a lot can be successfully accomplished by moving your doe, and your buck. You can insulate their pen, or move them to a heavier shaded area. You can also give them time in the great outdoors; every bunny loves yard time. Just make sure to remember to protect them from the direct sun, and make sure rain or snow isn't in the immediate forecast. Otherwise, allowing them time to enjoy all the fresh air, and fresh grass, that they want to take advantage of can greatly enhance their mood. You can also choose to put the pair together that you are wanting to mate, but make sure that you are nearby to supervise because if one becomes too aggressive, the other can end up being seriously injured. Plus, you will want to know if the breeding took place, so that you can mark it on your calendar and can be prepared when delivery time gets close. One downside of conjugal yard time is that if you don't have a lot of time, you may find yourself watching them chasing each other, or maybe even ignoring each other due to being in a different environment. Another downside is that if it is hot out, the chances of a successful mating is slim, even if they do decide to play nicely for a bit.

In regard to issues related to stress, these too can and should be addressed and kept in mind at all times, whether you are hoping for a mating or not. Conti are extremely susceptible to stress. If I have said it once, I have said it a trillion times: stress kills! That is true to humans and to rabbits. When it comes to breeding related issues though, stress can be a real deal breaker. If you suspect stress as being your hinderance to successfully breeding your pair, first eliminate the problem. Until you do, you are basically wasting your time doing anything else. By the way, if your rabbit is stressed, you will some of the things you may see are the rabbit being hunched up, not acting normally, avoiding contact with you, not eating normally, not drinking normally, showing signs of aggression, and sometimes there will be some foot-thumping when you attempt to force contact with them.

When it comes to age, there isn't much that can be done. Just about everyone you ask will offer their "expert opinion" of when the best age to begin breeding is. Some will say the bucks can or should be bred as soon as their testicles descend, others say doing so will stunt their growth. Some will tell you that does should not be bred before they are 9 or 10 months old, and others will tell you that they should be bred as soon as they turn 8 months old, and yes, some will tell you that you need to wait until the doe is over a year old before beginning. This is what I say: they are YOUR rabbits! No one knows your rabbits better than you do. As long as you are not pushing them just so that you can be selfish about having babies sooner, or still have the ridiculous idea in your head that you're going to get rich or make a lot of money from breeding them, then go with your gut instinct. Personally, I have seen it go both ways when it comes to the pre or post senior-age limit for breeding, and the best advice that I can offer you is to know your rabbit. Are they mature enough to deal with babies? Are they in top-notch healthy condition? Are they well fleshed and have good muscle tone? Do they eat well? If all the answers to these questions are yes, then good luck! If they are not ready to breed, nothing you do will make it happen. However, if they are ready and if they do breed, then the chances of the first breeding happening is about 50/50. This is especially true if you buck is young. Even though he may have 'dropped', it still may take some time for some potency to develop. Likewise, with your doe, if she does become pregnant at 8 months old, she may or may not know what to do with babies once they arrive. If that happens, don't hold it against her; but definitely consider waiting a while before you try to breed her again. If she is ready though, and does deliver a liter, she will intuitively begin building a nest and pulling fur before the birth occurs. If that doesn't happen, the chances are high that she may not take care of the babies. Furthermore, you may even discover that she had scattered the babies all over the floor of her enclosure. This alone could cause a lot of problems and is a strong indicator that she may not care for them; if she doesn't, they will not survive long unless you intervene - quickly. And of course, if you are breeding an older doe, she will reach the point when she stops producing. When that is the problem, it will not matter what you attempt to do, nothing will cause her to become pregnant. At that point, the best option is to allow her to live out the rest of her life as a dearly loved pet… either with you, or with someone else.

Next on the list is weight. An overweight doe will not produce a litter. You can breed her a hundred times; it will not happen. You can help her though, by providing more exercise, and less food. Give her some time and then try to breed her again. Unless she has been obese for quite a while, helping her shape up should improve the chances that she will produce a good litter for you. If it is your buck that is over-weight, well, it is not healthy, but he can still produce – if you can get him to breed the doe.

And finally, if your doe is being stubborn, well, welcome to the frustration of being a breeder. At one point or another, every breeder has experienced this to some degree. The good news is that there are some tricks of the trade that might make that job a little easier. Rather than repeating the entire list of tips, which was provided to you in the previous book, *Continental Giant Rabbits – Advanced tips for care, feeding, health, and housing,* I will just say that there are quite a few things you can try. The most common things are listed above. Otherwise, a few extra's are changing the location of the buck and doe, try breeding her to a different buck, decrease her feed intake for a couple days before breeding, and increase the lighting in her environment. Also, if it is hot weather, try breeding them indoors, where it is cooler; or putting a large fan in front of both, buck and doe, for a few days.

Additionally, I want to note here that just because your friend tells you that "this trick works every time", do not get discouraged if it doesn't happen when you do it. Remember, every Conti is different, so what works for one may not work at all for another. The most important thing, however, is that you do not give up. Be patient, and give it some time.

Continental Giant Rabbit Concerns

ELEVEN
Fur

Have you ever wondered what purpose fur serves for rabbits? If you have not, maybe you should take a moment to entertain the notions in the is section. Of course, there is the obvious reason of just making the bunnies cute, but that is not all that it does.

Fur is a method of protecting rabbits. It provides cushion to their feet, which prevents sore hocks. It also protects the skin from irritants and sun damage. Another benefit is that fur can also help the rabbit escape from some predators if they are being attacked. How is that, you may wonder? If the attacker does not get a good hold on the rabbit, the fur pulls out easily enough to allow the rabbit to get away – alive.

Warmth is also an obvious bonus in the cold winter months. In fact, rabbits deal with cold weather much better than they do heat because of their fur. Think about it; if you were wrapped from head to toe in a thick, dense layer of fur, would you be more comfortable in cooler temps, or when its hot? I sure wouldn't want to be in 80 degrees of heat if I were wrapped up in fur. When you add that kind of heat to the fact that rabbits do not have a built-in way to cool themselves, such as a dog does when he pants, the last thing I would want would be to that hot. However, on the flip side of that, newborns being born naked when they are designed to be wrapped up in all of that fur also could get equally as ugly. That is why even the slightest breeze of cool air, even on a hot day, could cause them to freeze to death. That is why the mom pulls so much fur when the babies are born; to keep them warm until their own fur starts to grow.

Here is something that you may not know about fur. Each breed has its' own type of fur, with specific length and density. Why is that important? It is important because knowing the fur your bunny has will also sometimes be a strong indicator of letting you know that your furry friend is sick. That's right! Because fur requires nutrients to be what it is, if you understand and pay attention to the quality of fur, you can learn a lot. For instance, if you feed is not providing the right nutrients, the fur will look different. If your bunny has stopped eating, you can also notice the fur will be dull in appearance. If your bunny is fighting an ear infection, as noted in the earlier chapter, one indication you may notice is that the fur will appear lifeless and, behind the ears, the fur may also feel or appear to look oily. If the fur looks fuzzy, this could be another warning sign that something is not quite right. Fur even has a way of remaining healthy, by shedding the dead coat and regrowth of a new coat; this is what we refer to as molting. By the way – it's called molting, not molding.

It is important that a rabbits' fur not get wet also. The reason is because wet fur promotes a whole host of problems, including but not limited to parasitic infestations and fly strike. Parasites are attracted to wet or damp, dark, warm places where they can lay their eggs. What better place than on a live host, where they can survive off of the animal they are born on. I won't go into the gory details, but I will say that if you ever have to deal with fly strike, it is not something that you will ever easily forget. It also can become deadly before you ever realize there is a problem, but hopefully, if you do ever have to experience this situation, you will catch it very early and will be able to save 'the host', aka your bunny.

Otherwise, fur does have other purposes as well; which you all know. Fur production is a lot of work, but can yield some absolutely beautiful items, such as blankets, pillows, coats, gloves, boots, and many other things. For the record though, Continental Giant's are not "fur producers". For that type of fur, the go-to breed would be an Angora – which is also commonly used for creating yarns used in making sweaters and other such clothing items.

TWELVE
Personality

If you have ever had the pleasure of spending time with a Continental Giant, you will quickly understand why they are so loved and desired. Not only does their size captivate you, but their intelligence will surprise you, and their personality will capture your heart. You may have even heard it said that "Conti are not for the faint of heart." That statement is one of the truest things ever spoken about this breed. The reason is because, since they so quickly capture your heart, they will equally crush your heart if you get one and it passes away. I have experienced and been told "never did I think that I would be so head-over-heals in love with a rabbit!" Trust me though, you will be! It happens before you realize it too.

Just as each dog, or human for that matter, has a specific personality – so do these rabbits. Some are down-right comical. They hop and bounce around like court-jesters on a mission. Others are more 'philosophical', as they look at you with their big beautiful eyes, you will quickly find yourself wondering just what is churning in that bunnies' brain. I have even had a Conti who loved nothing more than playing fetch. Yep! She was my all-star ballplayer. For as long as I would stand there and toss the ball to her, she would run to it, grab it with her teeth, and toss it back by flipping her head upwards and releasing the ball. There were times, too, when time was short and the game wasn't able to last very long. Can you guess what happened when I stopped playing before she was ready? Well, if you guessed that I got the proverbial cold-shoulder treatment, you guessed right. She would literally go to the back of her enclosure, turn her back to me, and blatantly ignore me. Sometimes, this little sassy attitude would go on for days, too. Other times, she would just stomp her foot and hop away; as if she were saying "fine! Be that way!"

That's not all either. Some does are 'born to be' moms and when they lose their babies, you can see it in their eyes that they are hurting, emotionally, due to the losses. I have had does that, if they lost a litter, they would stop eating and sulk for days. Others I have had would take such good care of their babies that they would refuse to eat until all the babies had eaten their fill. One doe I had, in particular, we had to separate her at feeding times once her babies got older because she would not eat at all, and would lose a lot of weight because of it. A few times, she would lose so much weight that we were concerned about her survival. If you have a doe like this, you will understand the importance of having separate areas set up to 'give mom a break.' By removing her from her babies, temporarily, it would give her time to rest a little bit and have the ability to eat freely – which should would then do, when her babies were not with her.

There are also the Conti which are referred to in some circles as being "royalty". These are the ones that give you the impression, on a regular basis, that they think of you as their servants; and heaven help you if you fail to perform correctly. They will often turn their backs to you, while glancing back over their shoulders to make sure that you are understanding that they are not one bit happy with you. These are also the ones who tend to show signs of jealousy. If you doubt that, just wait until you pay attention to a different pet before paying attention to him. I remember one buck who was so 'aristocratic' that if we so much as touched another rabbit before him, he would vocally grunt and refuse to eat until we 'payed our dues' and showered him with attention.

There are also the snuggle-bunnies. These are the ones who will often hop up in your lap, or lay down beside you, and will stay there for hours on end – as long as you will pay attention to them. These bunnies will steal your heart like none-other! They are often the ones that will also bump you with this nose when you're not giving them the attention they want, when they want it. Sometimes, when you're being a good human, they will even reward you by patting you with their front paw. That's a real treat!

There are other personalities as well, as many as you can think of, really, they exist. I'm sure that some of you may be thinking 'yeah, well, other breeds have personality too.' I'm not debating that they don't. However, until you have them and see for yourself, there really is no way to explain how clearly defined the Conti's personalities are. Some are picky eaters, others are super-clean freaks, and some are total slobs who just want to lounge around. Some of the bucks have what I can only describe as 'old-school-charm', too. They are flirts, and they let you know it. They will chin you every time you are near them, and often will circle your feet, as if to say "Hey you! Hey! The world revolved around me, but I will give you the moon if you spoil me just right."

I can not stress how important it is to shower your Conti with attention, either. From nearly the time they are born, they will single you out and draw you in. The more attention they are given, the sweeter they become, too. It's pretty easy to tell how much time that a breeder spends with their babies before they are sent to their new homes. The ones that don't get that attention still develop their own personality, but they seem more independent and less willing to compromise. For instance, they tend to develop an attitude of 'it's my way, or the highway' and often will hold a grudge longer when they are upset with you for some reason or another. The same is true with babies that came from a more hostile or less-than-nurturing environment. They will often be a bit jumpy and will startle easily, and sometimes will display signs of aggression. These are yet one more reason that those 'big breeders' who believe they need to have a barn loaded with Conti is not a good idea, and are often the ones that produce these babies-with-attitude. That is because, regardless of intention, there is no way that any human can provide that much time and attention to so many rabbits. Doing so would be a full day job, to say the very least. For the record, if you are wanting to avoid this type of thing, one way to find out who those 'big breeders' are is by paying attention to what and how often the person is advertising babies for sale. If they are cranking out one after the next, continually, the chance is high that they might have more bunnies in their barn than they can emotionally keep up with. That is not to say that those babies would be mean. I'm not saying that. What I am saying is that those babies might not have received the socialization that they need in order to become 'the sweetest baby', so to speak. Otherwise, I will also note here that genetics do play a part and I've watched several times when a breeder will continue breeding a Conti with a bad attitude, and that trait gets passed on to the offspring.

So, even though attention is vital, that is not the only reason that one personality may outshine another.

THIRTEEN
Medicine

In closing, I wanted to provide every person who reads this book with a list of what medicine is used for what problems. This is different that the previously given holistic list of help. This list is for medicine which is either prescribed by a Vet, or can be bought over the counter. I am not going to include dosage amounts, howver, because I am not a Vet and that information should be given to you by someone who is licensed to do that. Instead, the purpose of this list is to help you learn what the included types of medicines cover, and so that you can have a higher understanding of why your Vet may prescribe or suggest a certain type or brand of medicine, rather than something else you had thought might be given. Doing this, hopefully, will also give you something else to have an educated discussion with your Vet about, and perhaps will open the door towards you having an open and up-front discussion with your Vet. But always remember, at the end of the day, whatever you chose – the decision of what to give your rabbits is always your own decision yours to make.

If an item has an "*" by the name, there will be a comment with that item in regard to my own (or friends') personal experience with it; this is not to say that my experience is the bottom-line law of the land, either. Therefore, do not make it what it is not by putting words in place that I'm not saying. I will also say here – for about the 900-Millionth time – if you can treat with natural products, try it! Chemically based medicine, while it certainly has its uses, has the ability to, in the long run, cause more problems than what it fixes.

Albendazole: Antiparasitic

Albion*: Antiparasitic for coccidia

Amphotericin B: Antifungal (*only for severe fungal infections)

Amprolium*: Coccidiastat (*see Corid)

Aspirin*: Pain reliever (infant liquid Tylenol, or St. Joseph's chewable low dose tablets if over 12wks / not for pregnant or nursing does)

Aureomycin*: Antibiotic, used for bacterial and respiratory infections

Azithromycin (: Antibiotic, for abscesses and osteomyelitis

Bag Balm*: Topical Antiseptic Ointment, for sore hocks or wounds

Banamine: Pain reliever

Barium Suspension*: Anti-Diarrhea agent

Baycox: Coccidiastat / Antiparasitic, 99% parasite eradication (*also see Toltrazuril and Ponazuril)

Baytril*: Antibiotic, primarily used for infections of respiratory tract (*aka Enrofloxacin)

Benebac*: Probiotic, used to restore flora in gut

Bicillin*: Antibiotic (*see Pen-G and Dura-Pen)

Chloramphenicol: Antibiotic, for bacterial infection

Colloidal Silver (: (*also see Silver Sulfadiazine) Antibiotic Cream, for bacterial / fungal / viral infections ... also available as spray for use on nose, eyes, and ears. *known as the safest form of antibiotic

Calcium Drench*: induces labor, replaces calcium lost during birthing process, and assists with passing retained or mummified kits

Corid (Amprol / Amprolium)*: Cocccidiastat

Critical Care*: Nutritional Supplement

Diaepam: Sedative

Di-Methox: Antibiotic, for bacterial infections

Duramycin*: Antibiotic, (*see oxytetracyline)

Dura-Pen*: (Pen-G) Antibiotic, for bacterial infections

Fenbendazole*: Antiparasitic, for E.Cunniculi

Gentamicin: Eye drops, for Conjunctivitis

Imidacloprid: Flea eradication / topical treatment

Ivermec / Ivermectin*: Antiparasitic, for internal and external mites

LA-200*: Antibiotic, for bacterial and respiratory infections

Lactated Ringers*: (with Sterile Solution) IV Hydration

Marquis: Coccidiastat, offers 99.9% eradication

Metacam: Pain Reliever

Metronidazole: Antibiotic, for bacterial infection

Neosporin*: Topical Antibiotic ointment, for bacterial infections from abscesses and injuries

Neomycin Sulfate*: Antibacterial, for intestinal bacteria

Oxytetracycline*: Antibiotic, for viral and bacterial infections

Oxytocin*: Induces labor (*Very Strong) and aids in passing retained kits

Panacur*: Antiparasitic, for internal worms (effective for E. Cunniculi)

Pedialyte*: Electrolyte and Hydration replacement

Pepto Bismol*: Anti-Diarrhea agent

Pen-G*: Antibiotic (*see Dura-Pen)

Ponazuril: Coccidiastat / Antiparasitic, 99% parasite eradication (*also see Baycox and Toltrazuril)

Probios*: Probiotic, for digestive aide and restores gut flora

Reglan: Gut Mobility Stimulant, for upper GI tract stimulation

Safe-Guard*: Antiparasitic, for internal parasites

Silver Sulfadiazine*: Antibiotic (*see Colloidal Silver) *Highly effective and safe, with fast results

Sulmet*: Antibiotic, for bacterial and respiratory infection

Sulfaquinoxaline: Antiparasitic for coccidiosis

Tobramycin: Antibiotic, for bacterial eye infection

Terramycin*: Antibiotic ointment, for eye infections

Tetracycline*: Antibiotic

Vanodine* **– V18**: Biocide, for eradication of bacteria, fungus, and virus germs; also disinfects, sanitizes, sterilizes / can be used as foot bath, surface disinfectant, aerial disinfectant, added to drinking water, and sprayed in eyes, nose, mouth, and on open wounds. (*V18 is not available in the United States in pure form, however, there is a diluted form that can be found online)

Toltrazuril*: Coccidiastat / Antiparasitic, 99% parasite eradication (*also see Baycox and Ponazuril)

Note 1: Dosage is purposefully not provided for the reason of accepting zero responsibility or liability for the success or failure of your choice of use with any of the information contained here-within. To get the correct dosage amounts, speak to your exotic Vet and follow those guidelines.

Note 2: Make sure you follow directions given for any medications you are provided with. Failure to administer the correct dosage could be fatal to your bunny.

Disclaimer: All information contained within this section, or in other areas, is only provided for general informational purposes. This is not and should not replace the advice or guidance of a Veterinarian. Any information that you use which has been provided is solely at your own risk. No form of responsibility or liability of any kind is being offered.

Next on the list of medications is the often-asked question of "what does (xyz) mean?" How many times have you wondered what is the difference between ml and cc? Or maybe you have seen and wondered what 'amp' means. If so, you will find this part very much to your liking, as here is your reference to all of those abbreviated terms that you may be hearing about.

amp. – ampule

a.d. – right ear

a.s – left ear

a.u. – both ears

c. – with

cap. – capsule

disp. – dispense

gtt(s) – drop(s)

IM – intermuscular injection

IN – internasal

IP – intraperitoneal (within abdominal cavity)

IV – intravenous injection

o.d. – right eye

o.s. – left eye

o.u. – both eyes

PO – given orally / by mouth

q.s. = sufficient quantity

SubQ / SQ / SC – subcutaneous injection

Susp. – suspension

Tab – tablet

a.c. – before meals

p.c. – after meals

h. – hour

h.s. – bedtime

q. – every

SID – once daily

BID – twice daily

TID – three times daily

QID – four times daily

QOD – every other day

PRN – as needed

Sig. – directions were given

Stat – immediately

Ut. Dict. – as directed

And then, to take it one step further for those of you have hate math, or just may not know what the conversion of measurements are, this is for you.

Liquid Measurements:

1 milliliter / 1 mm = 1cc

1 teaspoon / 1 tsp = 5ml (5cc)

1 tablespoon / 1 Tbsp = 3 tsp = 14.79ml(cc) = ½ ounce(oz)

1 fluid ounce / 1 fl oz = 2 Tbsp = 29.57ml(cc)

1 cup / 1 cp = 16 Tbsp = 236.6ml(cc)

Weights:

1 microgram / 1 ug or mcg = 1,000 nanograms (ng)

1 milligram / 1 mg = 1,000 micrograms (uc/mcg)

1,000 mg = 1 gram(g) = 15.43 grains

1 grain (gr) = 64.8mg

1,000 g = 1 kilogram

1 kilogram(kg) = 2.2046 pounds (lbs) = 1,000 grams

1 pound (lb) = 0.4536 kg = 453.6 grams(g)

1 ounce (oz) = 28.35 grams(g)

FOURTEEN
Final Thoughts

In closing, if I could offer you but one piece of advice when it comes to coping with a sick rabbit, that advice is this: First and foremost, most importantly, do not panic!

Anytime that you think that this is a problem going on with your Continental Giant, first - take a deep breath, gather your senses, and then start at step one.

1. Do a visual & physical basic health check (head to toe)
2. Make note of anything that seems irregular, at all times, and do not ignore things that just don't seem quite normal
3. Never just start shoving food and meds into your rabbits

4. Know what your options are, before you need to use them
5. Have a mentor and an exotic vet – on speed dial
6. Know the number and location of a 24-hour emergency vet
7. Have every supply that you can get your hands on – on hand
8. Never be afraid to reach out for help
9. Keep a list of what dosages are for what homeopathic, over the counter, and prescription meds
10. Do NOT force-feed a rabbit with critical care or any other food item/product unless a Vet tells you to do so, and until you are fully aware of exactly what you are dealing with. Rabbits will not die if they do not eat for a day, or even two. Rabbits WILL die, however, if their GI tract is blocked and you continue to shove more foodstuff's into their already blocked gut and intestinal tracts. It is far more important to keep them hydrated.

Quick Tips:

- Papaya is stronger than Pineapple juice when it comes to a blocked gut
- Ginger Root is much faster acting and not chemically evasive when it comes to digestive aid
- Ginger Root is very spicey and strong; a SMALL amount is all you need

- Critical Care is not a 'cure all', every time your bunny gets an upset tummy. If you are going to use it – ensure you are using it properly, and do not OVER-use it.
- Any Chemically-based medication has the chance of causing further problems with the gut
- Always use a natural product if possible; this eliminates over-dosing and adverse side-effects resulting from the use of chemical medications
- Extra Virgin Olive Oil is the strongest, natural form of bacterial antibiotic for the GI Tract in existence. It can also be used externally for ear mite treatment, and orally as a laxative (SMALL amounts). Additionally, it can be used as a carrier-oil for diluting other products (ie: ginger root)
- Never assume that just because something works for one thing that it will absolutely work for everything. That's not the case.

Lastly – if you are seeking "expert advice", then seek an expert and keep in mind that not everyone who owns a rabbit and offers advice is that expert. In fact, unless someone has a bare minimum of 25 years of hands-on experience with raising rabbits, then I would personally not even consider them as knowing half of what they should know to be considered an expert. This is not being said to offend anyone. It is simply the truth in the respect that it takes MANY YEARS of knowledge and experience to know what you are doing, and even then, there are surprises waiting around every corner! Otherwise, if you need dosage amounts or other such information and do not have access to a Vet – at all – then there are many places online that you can look for that information. Find a reputable website… do not just assume that because Jane or John Doe told you it takes 3cc's of something then that is the law of the land. Everyone makes mistakes and everyone has a bad day, and it is super-easy to mistake ".1ml" for "1ml" – yet, just the omission or over-sight of the decimal point in that equation could quickly become a fatal mistake! So - Don't risk it! Therefore, also do not get huffy with others, or leave bad reviews about others, just because they (or I) have not given you dosage amounts. I, for one, am not a Vet, have never claimed to be one, and therefore, I am NOT willing to take on the liability of printing such information in this book, any other book, or on any other form of media, which then could easily result in human-error which would carry any chance of killing your rabbit. If you can't understand the ramifications of such… well… I highly suggest that ask yourself if you would take such a liability, because I highly doubt you would want the death of someone else's Conti resting on your shoulders, on the off chance that you might mistype or misquote something, or that someone else reading might mis-read it, and/or pass that information on to others.

Continental Giant Rabbit Concerns

Eva M. Wells

The following bonus section is for your own private records. These charts and forms may be filled out within the book, or printed for personal use ONLY. They may not be redistributed, copied, shared, or otherwise reproduced either mechanically nor digitally, without the express written permission of the author, Eva Wells.

Continental Giant Rabbit Concerns

*** BONUS SECTION ***

UN-OFFICIAL CONTI WEIGHT AND EAR-SIZE CHART- BASED ON FLEMISH GIANTS

(as of December 2020, there is no 'absolute' chart available for Conti)

AGE	WEIGHT	EAR LENGTH
1 MONTH	1.5 – 1.75	4"
1 MONTH 2 WEEKS	2.5 – 3.25	
2 MONTHS	4.0 – 4.75	5"
2 MONTH 2 WEEKS	5.5 – 5.75	
3 MONTHS	6.0 – 7.0	5.5"
3 MONTH 2 WEEKS	7.75 – 8.25	
4 MONTHS	9.25 – 9.50	5.75"
4 MONTH 2 WEEKS	10.0 – 10.25	
5 MONTHS	10.0 – 11.5	6"
5 MONTH 2 WEEKS	12.0 – 12.25	
6 MONTHS	12.25 – 13.0	7+
6 MONTH 2 WEEKS	13.0 – 13.50	
7 MONTHS	13.75 – 14.0	
7 MONTH 2 WEEKS	14.25 – 14.50	
8 MONTHS	14.50 – 15.0	
8 MONTH 2 WEEK	15.25 – 16.0	
9+ MONTHS	16 +	

GROWTH CHARTS

NAME:
DOB:
WEANED:

MONTHLY WEIGHTS

1M	2M	3M	4M	5M	6M	7M	8M	9M	12M
O	O	O	O	O	O	O	O	O	O

DAILY FEEDING CHART

AGE	HAY	PELLETS	FRUITS/ VEGGIES	NATURAL PLANTS
1MO				
2MO				
3MO				
4MO				
5MO				
6MO				
7MO				
8MO				
9MO				
10MO				
11MO				
12MO				

Continental Giant Rabbit Concerns

GROWTH CHARTS

NAME:
DOB:
WEANED:

MONTHLY WEIGHTS

1M	2M	3M	4M	5M	6M	7M	8M	9M	12M
O	O	O	O	O	O	O	O	O	O

DAILY FEEDING CHART

AGE	HAY	PELLETS	FRUITS/ VEGGIES	NATURAL PLANTS
1MO				
2MO				
3MO				
4MO				
5MO				
6MO				
7MO				
8MO				
9MO				
10MO				
11MO				
12MO				

Eva M. Wells

GROWTH CHARTS

NAME:
DOB:
WEANED:

MONTHLY WEIGHTS

1MO	2MO	3MO	4MO	5MO	6MO	7MO	8MO	9MO	12MO

DAILY FEEDING CHART

AGE	HAY	PELLETS	FRUITS/ VEGGIES	NATURAL PLANTS
1MO				
2MO				
3MO				
4MO				
5MO				
6MO				
7MO				
8MO				
9MO				
10MO				
11MO				
12MO				

GROWTH CHARTS

NAME:
DOB:
WEANED:

MONTHLY WEIGHTS

1M	2M	3M	4M	5M	6M	7M	8M	9M	12M
O	O	O	O	O	O	O	O	O	O

DAILY FEEDING CHART

AGE	HAY	PELLETS	FRUITS/ VEGGIES	NATURAL PLANTS
1MO				
2MO				
3MO				
4MO				
5MO				
6MO				
7MO				
8MO				
9MO				
10MO				
11MO				
12MO				

Track health concerns, treatments, and other important health-related notes about your own rabbits.

PERSONAL TREATMENT SCHEDULING NOTES

NAME:
DATE:
CONCERN:
TREATMENT:

NAME:
DATE:
CONCERN:
TREATMENT:

Track health concerns, treatments, and other important health-related notes about your own rabbits.

PERSONAL TREATMENT SCHEDULING NOTES

NAME:
DATE:
CONCERN:
TREATMENT:

NAME:
DATE:
CONCERN:
TREATMENT:

Track health concerns, treatments, and other important health-related notes about your own rabbits.

PERSONAL TREATMENT SCHEDULING NOTES

NAME:
DATE:
CONCERN:
TREATMENT:

NAME:
DATE:
CONCERN:
TREATMENT:

Continental Giant Rabbit Concerns

Track health concerns, treatments, and other important health-related notes about your own rabbits.

PERSONAL TREATMENT SCHEDULING NOTES

NAME:
DATE:
CONCERN:
TREATMENT:

NAME:
DATE:
CONCERN:
TREATMENT:

Track what you buy – including rabbits name, sex, dob, price, and misc. notes, from whom, and what method of transport is used or preferred by that breeder.

PREFERRED BREEDERS CONTACT INFORMATION

PERSONAL NAME:
RABBITRY NAME:
PHONE / EMAIL:
LOCATION:
PREFERRED TRANSPORT:
PURCHASE INFORMATION:

PERSONAL NAME:
RABBITRY NAME:
PHONE / EMAIL:
LOCATION:
PREFERRED TRANSPORT:
PURCHASE INFORMATION:

Continental Giant Rabbit Concerns

PREFERRED BREEDERS CONTACT INFORMATION

PERSONAL NAME:
RABBITRY NAME:
PHONE / EMAIL:
LOCATION:
PREFERRED TRANSPORT:
PURCHASE INFORMATION:

PERSONAL NAME:
RABBITRY NAME:
PHONE / EMAIL:
LOCATION:
PREFERRED TRANSPORT:
PURCHASE INFORMATION:

PREFERRED BREEDERS CONTACT INFORMATION

PERSONAL NAME:
RABBITRY NAME:
PHONE / EMAIL:
LOCATION:
PREFERRED TRANSPORT:
PURCHASE INFORMATION:

PERSONAL NAME:
RABBITRY NAME:
PHONE / EMAIL:
LOCATION:
PREFERRED TRANSPORT:
PURCHASE INFORMATION:

PREFERRED BREEDERS CONTACT INFORMATION

PERSONAL NAME:
RABBITRY NAME:
PHONE / EMAIL:
LOCATION:
PREFERRED TRANSPORT:
PURCHASE INFORMATION:

PERSONAL NAME:
RABBITRY NAME:
PHONE / EMAIL:
LOCATION:
PREFERRED TRANSPORT:
PURCHASE INFORMATION:

Track who you sell your rabbits to, for future references of purchase and recommendations to others who are interested in buying your bloodlines.

BUYERS CONTACT RECORDS

NAME:
PHONE / EMAIL:
LOCATION:
PREFERRED TRANSPORT:
RABBITS PURCHASED:

NAME:
PHONE / EMAIL:
LOCATION:
PREFERRED TRANSPORT:
RABBITS PURCHASED:

NAME:
PHONE / EMAIL:
LOCATION:
PREFERRED TRANSPORT:
RABBITS PURCHASED:

Continental Giant Rabbit Concerns

Track who you sell your rabbits to, for future references of purchase and recommendations to others who are interested in buying your bloodlines.

BUYERS CONTACT RECORDS

NAME:
PHONE / EMAIL:
LOCATION:
PREFERRED TRANSPORT:
RABBITS PURCHASED:

NAME:
PHONE / EMAIL:
LOCATION:
PREFERRED TRANSPORT:
RABBITS PURCHASED:

NAME:
PHONE / EMAIL:
LOCATION:
PREFERRED TRANSPORT:
RABBITS PURCHASED:

Eva M. Wells

Track who you sell your rabbits to, for future references of purchase and recommendations to others who are interested in buying your bloodlines.

BUYERS CONTACT RECORDS

NAME:
PHONE / EMAIL:
LOCATION:
PREFERRED TRANSPORT:
RABBITS PURCHASED:

NAME:
PHONE / EMAIL:
LOCATION:
PREFERRED TRANSPORT:
RABBITS PURCHASED:

NAME:
PHONE / EMAIL:
LOCATION:
PREFERRED TRANSPORT:
RABBITS PURCHASED:

Continental Giant Rabbit Concerns

Track who you sell your rabbits to, for future references of purchase and recommendations to others who are interested in buying your bloodlines.

BUYERS CONTACT RECORDS

NAME:
PHONE / EMAIL:
LOCATION:
PREFERRED TRANSPORT:
RABBITS PURCHASED:

NAME:
PHONE / EMAIL:
LOCATION:
PREFERRED TRANSPORT:
RABBITS PURCHASED:

NAME:
PHONE / EMAIL:
LOCATION:
PREFERRED TRANSPORT:
RABBITS PURCHASED:

Track who you sell your rabbits to, for future references of purchase and recommendations to others who are interested in buying your bloodlines.

BUYERS CONTACT RECORDS

NAME:
PHONE / EMAIL:
LOCATION:
PREFERRED TRANSPORT:
RABBITS PURCHASED:

NAME:
PHONE / EMAIL:
LOCATION:
PREFERRED TRANSPORT:
RABBITS PURCHASED:

NAME:
PHONE / EMAIL:
LOCATION:
PREFERRED TRANSPORT:
RABBITS PURCHASED:

Continental Giant Rabbit Concerns

DO NOT SELL TO LIST

PERSONAL NAME:
RABBITRY NAME:
LOCATION:
REASON:

PERSONAL NAME:
RABBITRY NAME:
LOCATION:
REASON:

PERSONAL NAME:
RABBITRY NAME:
LOCATION:
REASON:

PERSONAL NAME:
RABBITRY NAME:
LOCATION:
REASON:

PERSONAL NAME:
RABBITRY NAME:
LOCATION:
REASON:

Eva M. Wells

DO NOT SELL TO LIST

PERSONAL NAME:
RABBITRY NAME:
LOCATION:
REASON:

PERSONAL NAME:
RABBITRY NAME:
LOCATION:
REASON:

PERSONAL NAME:
RABBITRY NAME:
LOCATION:
REASON:

PERSONAL NAME:
RABBITRY NAME:
LOCATION:
REASON:

PERSONAL NAME:
RABBITRY NAME:
LOCATION:
REASON:

Continental Giant Rabbit Concerns

DO NOT BUY FROM LIST

PERSONAL NAME:
RABBITRY NAME:
LOCATION:
REASON:

PERSONAL NAME:
RABBITRY NAME:
LOCATION:
REASON:

PERSONAL NAME:
RABBITRY NAME:
LOCATION:
REASON:

PERSONAL NAME:
RABBITRY NAME:
LOCATION:
REASON:

PERSONAL NAME:
RABBITRY NAME:
LOCATION:
REASON:

Eva M. Wells

DO NOT BUY FROM LIST

PERSONAL NAME:
RABBITRY NAME:
LOCATION:
REASON:

PERSONAL NAME:
RABBITRY NAME:
LOCATION:
REASON:

PERSONAL NAME:
RABBITRY NAME:
LOCATION:
REASON:

PERSONAL NAME:
RABBITRY NAME:
LOCATION:
REASON:

PERSONAL NAME:
RABBITRY NAME:
LOCATION:
REASON:

Continental Giant Rabbit Concerns

BLOODLINES WITH KNOWN GENETIC DISORDERS

BREEDER'S RABBITRY / PERSONAL NAME:

BREEDERS' LOCATION:

RABBIT'S LINEAGE / NAMES INVOLVED:

GENETIC DISORDER:

(If not self-discovered) INFORMED OF DISORDER BY:

RECOMMENDATION FOR DEALING WITH DISORDER:

      SOFT CULL ____   HARD CULL ____   N/A ____

MISC. NOTES:

BREEDER'S RABBITRY / PERSONAL NAME:

BREEDERS' LOCATION:

RABBIT'S LINEAGE / NAMES INVOLVED:

GENETIC DISORDER:

(If not self-discovered) INFORMED OF DISORDER BY:

RECOMMENDATION FOR DEALING WITH DISORDER:

      SOFT CULL ____   HARD CULL ____   N/A ____

MISC. NOTES:

BLOODLINES WITH KNOWN GENETIC DISORDERS

BREEDER'S RABBITRY / PERSONAL NAME:

BREEDERS' LOCATION:

RABBIT'S LINEAGE / NAMES INVOLVED:

GENETIC DISORDER:

(If not self-discovered) INFORMED OF DISORDER BY:

RECOMMENDATION FOR DEALING WITH DISORDER:

      SOFT CULL ____ HARD CULL ____ N/A ____

MISC. NOTES:

BREEDER'S RABBITRY / PERSONAL NAME:

BREEDERS' LOCATION:

RABBIT'S LINEAGE / NAMES INVOLVED:

GENETIC DISORDER:

(If not self-discovered) INFORMED OF DISORDER BY:

RECOMMENDATION FOR DEALING WITH DISORDER:

      SOFT CULL ____ HARD CULL ____ N/A ____

MISC. NOTES:

Continental Giant Rabbit Concerns

BLOODLINES WITH KNOWN GENETIC DISORDERS

BREEDER'S RABBITRY / PERSONAL NAME:

BREEDERS' LOCATION:

RABBIT'S LINEAGE / NAMES INVOLVED:

GENETIC DISORDER:

(If not self-discovered) INFORMED OF DISORDER BY:

RECOMMENDATION FOR DEALING WITH DISORDER:

      SOFT CULL ____ HARD CULL ____ N/A ____

MISC. NOTES:

BREEDER'S RABBITRY / PERSONAL NAME:

BREEDERS' LOCATION:

RABBIT'S LINEAGE / NAMES INVOLVED:

GENETIC DISORDER:

(If not self-discovered) INFORMED OF DISORDER BY:

RECOMMENDATION FOR DEALING WITH DISORDER:

      SOFT CULL ____ HARD CULL ____ N/A ____

MISC. NOTES:

BLOODLINES WITH KNOWN GENETIC DISORDERS

BREEDER'S RABBITRY / PERSONAL NAME:

BREEDERS' LOCATION:

RABBIT'S LINEAGE / NAMES INVOLVED:

GENETIC DISORDER:

(If not self-discovered) INFORMED OF DISORDER BY:

RECOMMENDATION FOR DEALING WITH DISORDER:

      SOFT CULL ____ HARD CULL ____ N/A ____

MISC. NOTES:

BREEDER'S RABBITRY / PERSONAL NAME:

BREEDERS' LOCATION:

RABBIT'S LINEAGE / NAMES INVOLVED:

GENETIC DISORDER:

(If not self-discovered) INFORMED OF DISORDER BY:

RECOMMENDATION FOR DEALING WITH DISORDER:

      SOFT CULL ____ HARD CULL ____ N/A ____

MISC. NOTES:

PERSONAL BREEDING GOALS

Use this for planning how to increase specific traits in specific rabbits, such as what strengths to breed to what weaknesses to improve the outcome in the offspring.

PERSONAL BREEDING GOALS

Use this for planning how to increase specific traits in specific rabbits, such as what strengths to breed to what weaknesses to improve the outcome in the offspring.

Continental Giant Rabbit Concerns

PERSONAL BREEDING GOALS

Use this for planning how to increase specific traits in specific rabbits, such as what strengths to breed to what weaknesses to improve the outcome in the offspring.

PERSONAL BREEDING GOALS

Use this for planning how to increase specific traits in specific rabbits, such as what strengths to breed to what weaknesses to improve the outcome in the offspring.

Continental Giant Rabbit Concerns

RABBIT EMERGENCY CONTACT LIST

NAME:
EXOTIC VET __ TRADITIONAL VET ___ BREEDER __
CONTACT:
LOCATION:
NOTES:

NAME:
EXOTIC VET __ TRADITIONAL VET __ BREEDER ___
CONTACT:
LOCATION:
NOTES:

NAME:
EXOTIC VET __ TRADITIONAL VET ___ BREEDER __
CONTACT:
LOCATION:
NOTES:

RABBIT EMERGENCY CONTACT LIST

NAME:
EXOTIC VET __ TRADITIONAL VET ___ BREEDER __
CONTACT:
LOCATION:
NOTES:

NAME:
EXOTIC VET __ TRADITIONAL VET ___ BREEDER __
CONTACT:
LOCATION:
NOTES:

NAME:
EXOTIC VET __ TRADITIONAL VET ___ BREEDER __
CONTACT:
LOCATION:
NOTES:

Continental Giant Rabbit Concerns

VACCINE RECORDS

RABBITS NAME:
DATE OF BIRTH:
VACCINE NAME:
DATE(s) OF VACCINE:
VACCINE GIVEN BY:
REACTIONS / NOTES:

RABBITS NAME:
DATE OF BIRTH:
VACCINE NAME:
DATE(s) OF VACCINE:
VACCINE GIVEN BY:
REACTIONS / NOTES:

RABBITS NAME:
DATE OF BIRTH:
VACCINE NAME:
DATE(s) OF VACCINE:
VACCINE GIVEN BY:
REACTIONS / NOTES:

Eva M. Wells

VACCINE RECORDS

RABBITS NAME:
DATE OF BIRTH:
VACCINE NAME:
DATE(s) OF VACCINE:
VACCINE GIVEN BY:
REACTIONS / NOTES:

RABBITS NAME:
DATE OF BIRTH:
VACCINE NAME:
DATE(s) OF VACCINE:
VACCINE GIVEN BY:
REACTIONS / NOTES:

RABBITS NAME:
DATE OF BIRTH:
VACCINE NAME:
DATE(s) OF VACCINE:
VACCINE GIVEN BY:
REACTIONS / NOTES:

Continental Giant Rabbit Concerns

VACCINE RECORDS

RABBITS NAME:
DATE OF BIRTH:
VACCINE NAME:
DATE(s) OF VACCINE:
VACCINE GIVEN BY:
REACTIONS / NOTES:

RABBITS NAME:
DATE OF BIRTH:
VACCINE NAME:
DATE(s) OF VACCINE:
VACCINE GIVEN BY:
REACTIONS / NOTES:

RABBITS NAME:
DATE OF BIRTH:
VACCINE NAME:
DATE(s) OF VACCINE:
VACCINE GIVEN BY:
REACTIONS / NOTES:

VACCINE RECORDS

RABBITS NAME:
DATE OF BIRTH:
VACCINE NAME:
DATE(s) OF VACCINE:
VACCINE GIVEN BY:
REACTIONS / NOTES:

RABBITS NAME:
DATE OF BIRTH:
VACCINE NAME:
DATE(s) OF VACCINE:
VACCINE GIVEN BY:
REACTIONS / NOTES:

RABBITS NAME:
DATE OF BIRTH:
VACCINE NAME:
DATE(s) OF VACCINE:
VACCINE GIVEN BY:
REACTIONS / NOTES:

Continental Giant Rabbit Concerns

TREATMENT RECORDS

RABBITS NAME:
DATE OF BIRTH:

MEDICATION NAME:
MEDICATION DATE & TIME GIVEN:
MEDICATION GIVEN BY: TOPICAL _____ ORAL_____ SUB-Q_____   IM_____
REACTIONS / NOTES:

MEDICATION NAME:
MEDICATION DATE & TIME GIVEN:
MEDICATION GIVEN BY: TOPICAL _____ ORAL_____ SUB-Q_____   IM_____
REACTIONS / NOTES:

MEDICATION NAME:
MEDICATION DATE & TIME GIVEN:
MEDICATION GIVEN BY: TOPICAL _____ ORAL_____ SUB-Q_____   IM_____
REACTIONS / NOTES:

MEDICATION NAME:
MEDICATION DATE & TIME GIVEN:
MEDICATION GIVEN BY: TOPICAL _____ ORAL_____ SUB-Q_____   IM_____
REACTIONS / NOTES:

Eva M. Wells

TREATMENT RECORDS

RABBITS NAME:
DATE OF BIRTH:

MEDICATION NAME:
MEDICATION DATE & TIME GIVEN:
MEDICATION GIVEN BY: TOPICAL _____ ORAL_____ SUB-Q_____ IM_____
REACTIONS / NOTES:

MEDICATION NAME:
MEDICATION DATE & TIME GIVEN:
MEDICATION GIVEN BY: TOPICAL _____ ORAL_____ SUB-Q_____ IM_____
REACTIONS / NOTES:

MEDICATION NAME:
MEDICATION DATE & TIME GIVEN:
MEDICATION GIVEN BY: TOPICAL _____ ORAL_____ SUB-Q_____ IM_____
REACTIONS / NOTES:

MEDICATION NAME:
MEDICATION DATE & TIME GIVEN:
MEDICATION GIVEN BY: TOPICAL _____ ORAL_____ SUB-Q_____ IM_____
REACTIONS / NOTES:

Continental Giant Rabbit Concerns

TREATMENT RECORDS

RABBITS NAME:
DATE OF BIRTH:

MEDICATION NAME:
MEDICATION DATE & TIME GIVEN:
MEDICATION GIVEN BY: TOPICAL____ ORAL____ SUB-Q____ IM____
REACTIONS / NOTES:

MEDICATION NAME:
MEDICATION DATE & TIME GIVEN:
MEDICATION GIVEN BY: TOPICAL____ ORAL____ SUB-Q____ IM____
REACTIONS / NOTES:

MEDICATION NAME:
MEDICATION DATE & TIME GIVEN:
MEDICATION GIVEN BY: TOPICAL____ ORAL____ SUB-Q____ IM____
REACTIONS / NOTES:

MEDICATION NAME:
MEDICATION DATE & TIME GIVEN:
MEDICATION GIVEN BY: TOPICAL____ ORAL____ SUB-Q____ IM____
REACTIONS / NOTES:

Eva M. Wells

TREATMENT RECORDS

RABBITS NAME:
DATE OF BIRTH:

MEDICATION NAME:
MEDICATION DATE & TIME GIVEN:
MEDICATION GIVEN BY: TOPICAL _____ ORAL _____ SUB-Q _____ IM _____
REACTIONS / NOTES:

MEDICATION NAME:
MEDICATION DATE & TIME GIVEN:
MEDICATION GIVEN BY: TOPICAL _____ ORAL _____ SUB-Q _____ IM _____
REACTIONS / NOTES:

MEDICATION NAME:
MEDICATION DATE & TIME GIVEN:
MEDICATION GIVEN BY: TOPICAL _____ ORAL _____ SUB-Q _____ IM _____
REACTIONS / NOTES:

MEDICATION NAME:
MEDICATION DATE & TIME GIVEN:
MEDICATION GIVEN BY: TOPICAL _____ ORAL _____ SUB-Q _____ IM _____
REACTIONS / NOTES:

Continental Giant Rabbit Concerns

TREATMENT RECORDS

RABBITS NAME:
DATE OF BIRTH:

MEDICATION NAME:
MEDICATION DATE & TIME GIVEN:
MEDICATION GIVEN BY: TOPICAL ____ ORAL____ SUB-Q ____ IM ____
REACTIONS / NOTES:

MEDICATION NAME:
MEDICATION DATE & TIME GIVEN:
MEDICATION GIVEN BY: TOPICAL ____ ORAL____ SUB-Q ____ IM ____
REACTIONS / NOTES:

MEDICATION NAME:
MEDICATION DATE & TIME GIVEN:
MEDICATION GIVEN BY: TOPICAL ____ ORAL____ SUB-Q ____ IM ____
REACTIONS / NOTES:

MEDICATION NAME:
MEDICATION DATE & TIME GIVEN:
MEDICATION GIVEN BY: TOPICAL ____ ORAL____ SUB-Q ____ IM ____
REACTIONS / NOTES:

Eva M. Wells

TREATMENT RECORDS

RABBITS NAME:
DATE OF BIRTH:

MEDICATION NAME:
MEDICATION DATE & TIME GIVEN:
MEDICATION GIVEN BY: TOPICAL ____ ORAL ____ SUB-Q ____ IM ____
REACTIONS / NOTES:

MEDICATION NAME:
MEDICATION DATE & TIME GIVEN:
MEDICATION GIVEN BY: TOPICAL ____ ORAL ____ SUB-Q ____ IM ____
REACTIONS / NOTES:

MEDICATION NAME:
MEDICATION DATE & TIME GIVEN:
MEDICATION GIVEN BY: TOPICAL ____ ORAL ____ SUB-Q ____ IM ____
REACTIONS / NOTES:

MEDICATION NAME:
MEDICATION DATE & TIME GIVEN:
MEDICATION GIVEN BY: TOPICAL ____ ORAL ____ SUB-Q ____ IM ____
REACTIONS / NOTES:

Continental Giant Rabbit Concerns

IN THE EVENT OF MY DEATH,
PLEASE FOLLOW THESE INSTRUCTIONS FOR MY RABBITS (PAGE 1)

PLEASE SELL / GIVE MY RABBITS TO:
BREED 1: PERSON: AT:
BREED 2: PERSON: AT:
BREED 3: PERSON: AT:

PLEASE SELL / GIVE MY CAGES TO:
PERSON 1: AT:
PERSON 2: AT:
PERSON 3: AT:

PLEASE SELL / GIVE MY MISC. EQUIPTMENT TO:
PERSON 1: AT:
PERSON 2: AT:
PERSON 3: AT:

PASSWORD TO MY PEDIGREE SOFTWARE IS: _____
PASSWORD TO COMPUTER / PHONE IS: _____
I DO / DO NOT WANT PEDIGREES TO BE GIVEN WITH RABBITS.
BREED _____
- SR. BUCKS $_____ SR. DOES $_____ JUNIORS $_____
BREED _____
- SR. BUCKS $_____ SR. DOES $_____ JUNIORS $_____
BREED _____
- SR. BUCKS $_____ SR. DOES $_____ JUNIORS $_____

Eva M. Wells

IN THE EVENT OF MY DEATH, PLEASE FOLLOW THESE INSTRUCTIONS FOR MY RABBITS (PAGE 2)

CAGE SIZE _____ price $_____

CAGE SIZE _____ price $_____

CAGE SIZE _____ price $_____

CARRIER SIZE _____ price $_____

CARRIER SIZE _____ price $_____

CARRIER SIZE _____ price $_____

MISC. EQUIPTMENT_____ price $_____

MISC. EQUIPTMENT_____ price $_____

MISC. EQUIPTMENT_____ price $_____

OTHER SPECIAL INSTRUCTIONS:

SIGNATURE: _____

DATE: _____

PERSONAL NOTES

Eva M. Wells

PERSONAL NOTES

Continental Giant Rabbit Concerns

PERSONAL NOTES

Eva M. Wells

PERSONAL NOTES

Eva M. Wells is the author of the first books ever published for Continental Giants. As an extension to her first two books, *Continental Giant Rabbits in USA; The ultimate guide for breeders, exhibitors, and pet owners*, and *Continental Giant Rabbits; Advanced tips for care, feeding, housing, and health*. She is taking the next step in this book by providing more extensive information to cover some of the most common health concerns of the world-renown breed, Continental Giant Rabbits.

Eva M. Wells is known as a leading adviser and mentor to many Conti owners. She has also developed and/or created the content for many large public and private rabbit-based websites, social media forums, and much more. She has worked diligently with local and state officials in legal capacities, offered informative and well researched advice to Veterinarians, and assisted a vast number of breeders and pet owners with care, health, identifications, and various other topics relating to these gentle giants. Additionally, she is the creator of the Continental Giant Rabbit Convention in USA, which is an annual event provided for educational purposes of this breed.

If you are interested in promoting the Continental Giant rabbit breed, two positive impacts that you can make is by kindly providing a review for this and the other two books in this series, and by giving these books as gifts to others interested in owning this breed – or suggesting to them the location of where and how they may obtain the books for themselves.

BOOKS IN THIS SERIES:

BOOK 1: Continental Giants in USA – The ultimate guide for breeders, exhibitors, and pet owners

BOOK 2: Continental Giant Rabbits – Advanced tips for care, feeding, health, and housing

BOOK 3: Giant Continental Concerns – Health matters

Children's books by this author:

Jester's 1st Christmas

**PLEASE TAKE A MOMENT
AND KINDLY LEAVE A REVIEW FOR THIS BOOK,
WHERE YOU PURCHASED IT FROM.**

Thanks in advance

Continental Giant Rabbit Concerns

If you have questions about Continental Giants, please refer to the website:

https://www.continentalgiantusa.com

To connect with other Continental Giant owners and breeders, please join our face book page at:

https://www.facebook.com/groups/continentalgiantsinusa

To purchase other books by this author, please visit the Amazon Author Page at:

https://www.amazon.com/Eva-Wells/e/B08G8Y1Y5P?ref_=dbs_p_pbk_r00_abau_000000

To connect directly with the author, please contact her at:

http://www.1stchoicehypnosis.com

Every day is a new chance to write a better story - EMW